WALKING IN THE SPIRIT

WALKING IN THE SPIRIT

Michael Harper

BETHANY HOUSE PUBLISHERS
MINNEAPOLIS, MINNESOTA 55438
A Division of Bethany Fellowship, Inc.

Published by Bethany House Publishers
A Division of Bethany Fellowship, Inc.
6820 Auto Club Road, Minneapolis, MN 55438

Printed in the United States of America

Contents

1. Hidden Treasure 13
2. The Missing Link 20
3. Seeing the Promise 27
4. Receiving the Promise 39
5. Living on the Promises 68
6. When You Come Together 84
7. Members One of Another 93
8. Weak Though Anointed 101
9. It Happened to Me 106
   Notes 111
   Further Reading 112

Publisher's Note

Michael Harper, for many years a well-loved and respected leader in the Charismatic Renewal, wrote his first book on the subject of the baptism with the Holy Spirit in 1964—*Power for the Body of Christ*. This original study makes up the first five chapters of this book and also Chapter Nine. Chapters Six through Eight are from his book entitled *Walk in the Spirit*, originally published in England in 1968.

Introduction

Over 20 years ago my wife and I became closely associated with what has come to be called 'the charismatic renewal.' We have seen it mushroom up in the middle of our present church situations. To some it is exciting, but to others it is bewildering in its comparative novelty. One common feature is the reappearance of the miraculous powers which marked the early days of the Christian church. But there is an almost complete absence of the hysteria usually associated with these things. It is coming into the experiences of people of different classes, races and denominations. But it is much more than a renewal of the miraculous; there is a profounder love and joy radiating from these people. Christians are becoming more like the kind of people Paul wrote his letters to—yes, their faults as well as their virtues.

The purpose of writing this book is to try to help those who have come into touch with this new dimension. It may seem strange to those who so far do not understand the background. A car salesman does not give the handbook to a potential customer—with its detailed instructions about the electrical circuits and the kind of lubricant to use. Instead he will give him a glossy leaflet which informs him of the main advantages of the car. This book is mainly like the car handbook. It explains how to keep it running smoothly, and how to repair it if it breaks down. Nevertheless the first chapter is more like the glossy hand-out of the car salesman. It may help you to decide to become part of this move of God's Spirit. It has deliberately been included for those who would like to know what the great experience of the Holy Spirit is, and how one can receive it. Other books have been written, if you should want to study the background to this whole subject, with accounts of people's experiences and how these blessings have come to churches. A few of these are listed at the end of this book.

Dr Fison has written:

> The story of Acts is the story of stupendous missionary achievement of a community inspired to make a continual series of creative experiments by the Pentecostal Spirit. Against a static church, unwilling to obey the guidance of the Spirit, no 'gates' of any sort are needed to oppose its movement, *for it does not move*. But against a church that is on the move, inspired by the Pentecostal Spirit, neither 'the gates of hell' nor any other gates can prevail.[1]

The early Christians knew what was meant by the term 'the fullness of the Holy Spirit'. When they came to appoint men to 'serve tables', they picked 'seven men of good repute, full of the Holy Spirit and of wisdom' (Acts 6:3). The apostles Peter and John detected something that was deficient in the experience of the new converts in Samaria, and so prayed that 'they might receive the Holy Spirit' (Acts 8:15). We may perhaps conjecture that a similarly obvious deficiency caused Paul to ask the disciples of John the Baptist in Ephesus the leading question, 'Did you receive the Holy Spirit when you believed?' (Acts 19:2). Lesslie Newbigin has put it very well:

> Theologians today are afraid of the word 'experience'. I do not think it is possible to survey this New Testament evidence... without recognising that the New Testament writers are free from this fear. They regard the gift of the Holy Spirit as an event which can be unmistakably recognised.[2]

It is equally clear from the New Testament that the early Christian fellowships were richly endowed with spiritual gifts. Even when writing to the carnal church at Corinth Paul acknowledged that they were 'not lacking in any spiritual gift' (1 Cor 1:7). He expected every member of the church to manifest at least one of these gifts 'for the common good', and indeed urged them to bring their spiritual gifts to church with them. They seemed more concerned in those days with this kind of gift than with taking up collections.

The Acts of the Apostles makes embarrassing reading today, if we are right in believing that our churches should bear some resemblance to those early ones. The church expanded in those days with a rapidity which shames most modern evangelism, in spite of all its up-to-date techniques and novel methods of mass communication. Only in the third world is anything comparable taking place, and it is not without significance that it is being done largely through

11

Pentecostals, who recognize the importance of the Holy Spirit, and accept the gifts of the Spirit in their community life. The early Christians healed the sick and cast out evil spirits as an integral part of the gospel of the kingdom. In this they were following the example of their Master. It was not just a 'battle for the mind', but a conflict involving the whole personality.

Thank God, we are seeing in our day the renewal of spiritual power in the lives of many Christians. It is springing from the recognition by many that we do not know the Holy Spirit as we should, and that it is possible, indeed imperative, to be filled with the Holy Spirit, and led by him as the early Christians were. We do need a breath of fresh air, and as God sends it, so it will blow away many ecclesiastical cobwebs. This book is written to show how, having this experience, and avoiding the dangerous shoals, we can steer a straight course as the Spirit himself directs.

1

Hidden Treasure

There is a story about an old Roman Catholic priest in a parish on the west coast of Ireland. He was wrestling with two problems at once, having to cope with the new liturgy in English and with a new public address system that had been installed in his church. In the middle of one of the services he tapped a troublesome microphone and said to the congregation, 'This thing does not work,'—to which his congregation replied spontaneously, 'And also with you.'

It isn't only p.a. systems that don't work in our churches. There is something more radically wrong than that, and the surfeit of new services, organizations and clever ideas has done little to remedy the situation. The problem is still an absence of *power* in the lives of Christians.

I say 'still', because I first wrote on this subject in 1964 and my convictions have not wavered since then. The problem is as acute today as it was then. But throughout the intervening years men and women in the millions have discovered that the experience that the early Christians had at Pentecost is still available and that Jesus Christ still baptizes his people with the Holy Spirit.

13

The charismatic renewal in 1964 was in its infancy, and you could count the numbers who had been filled with the Holy Spirit in thousands. It was before the Roman Catholic renewal began (in 1967). But the growth rate since then has been spectacular and now the figures reach into the millions, and it is still growing fast. The younger generation are wanting to know also about this promise of power.

I wrote this book because of my conviction that the churches were leaving out something very important. I wrote it also because in September 1962 my wife and I had an experience which changed our lives. We have never been the same since. During that month I was invited to speak at a parish weekend at Farnham in Surrey. They asked me to speak on the Epistle to the Ephesians. Little did I know at the time that this weekend was going to transform my Christian life in a radical fashion.

I had become a Christian while an undergraduate studying law at Cambridge in the fifties. I had entrusted my life to Jesus Christ and surrendered to him as Lord. I ended up studying theology and being ordained as a Church of England minister.

As I studied what Paul wrote to the Ephesians I became aware that God was speaking to me in a direct way. I realized that Paul prayed two prayers in his letter, one in chapter 1 and the other in chapter 3. God seemed to be shining a spotlight on these two prayers. I realized that they had two main themes; the first was that we might *know*, and the second that we might *have*. It was obvious also that he was praying for *Christians* not for unbelievers.

What did he want us to know and to have? The first

prayer clearly was for revelation about who we are and what we are capable of achieving in Christ; what our hope is, what our 'riches' are, and what his power is. I began to realize that there was so much I ought to know and didn't; that I was living in comparative spiritual poverty because I was ignorant of all that was available in Christ. But in the second prayer Paul prays that Christians might 'get it'. The link between the two prayers is most important. We won't receive without asking, but it's no good asking if we don't know what to ask for. The first prayer seemed to be a revelation of what to ask for, what is available to us in Christ and what we ought to be in him. The second prayer seemed to me at the time to be saying, 'Now, come and get it.'

The only problem I had when I left our flat in London's West End was whether this was for me or not. I had read books about great Christian leaders who had received deep experiences of God, and it seemed that they needed it. But what about me? I was an unknown disciple who was reasonably contented as a Christian, happily married and in an enjoyable and fulfilling job.

It was as my train to Farnham threaded its way through the maze of points outside Waterloo station that the truth dawned on me. In Ephesians 3:18 Paul's prayer was 'for all the saints', and although I didn't feel much like a saint I knew enough about the New Testament to realize that it meant me, because the word 'saint' means 'Christian'. It was for all God's people, even me.

Now, deep though my experience of God had been since I was 'born again' at Cambridge in 1951, I certainly could not say that I knew what it was to be 'filled with all the fullness of God' as Paul states in Ephesians

3:19. *Yet it was for me*, and for the first time I began to experience it during the weekend at Farnham. Whatever others may have thought about what I was saying that weekend, I listened to myself with mounting excitement. I was saying and believing all kinds of things that had never crossed my mind before. I found one other fascinating thing was happening too: I didn't seem to be boring the audience. They too were listening and I was going on longer than I normally did.

When I got home I shared it with my wife, but was wise enough not to be too enthusiastic. I then came to the conclusion that she had realized this for a long time and had only been prevented from experiencing it because she was married to a clergyman who was meant to know his theology. I had been able to put off my wife with theological excuses when she asked me embarrassing questions like, 'Why don't we experience the same things that the apostles did?' and, 'What does it really mean to be filled with the Holy Spirit?'

But Jeanne was not going to be cheated any longer. She was wanting the same thing that I had found that weekend—and the following Thursday she too received. In the meantime I had bought her a new Bible suitably inscribed which I gave her that evening.

The next step for us was to try to come to understand what had happened to us. I decided to study nothing but the Bible for the next few months. We were amazed at what we found. We realized we had stumbled on lost treasure. There hidden in the Scriptures was a promise for Christians which ignorance and prejudice had hidden from us all these years. Now the treasure was glinting in the sunlight.

As we examined our Bibles it began to dawn on us

16

that this was the missing link. Here was one of the secrets of the early church's amazing growth and inspiration. Here was how they became so convinced about the truth that they were prepared to die for it. Here was God's answer for them when they were persecuted and martyred. This was the key to their success in evangelism, and the secret of their worship. After all, it was what had been promised to them by the Lord Jesus Christ. It was his final message to them before he was taken up to heaven and they saw him no more.

But how could we put this to the test? How were we to know that what had worked for us would work for others? A few weeks after this experience Kathleen telephoned us. She had heard on the grapevine that we were mysteriously different. Could she come and talk to us and would we pray for her too? We had never done such a thing before, but we were prepared to talk about it with her. When it came to it we were very nervous. We tried hard to think of other people who could pray for her. But Kathleen made up our minds for us. She slipped forward on to her knees. Jeanne stood behind her and gently laid her hands on her head; we did not really expect anything to happen. She was 'overwhelmed' by the Spirit and lay seemingly unconscious. We had never seen anything like this happen before and were not sure how to handle the situation. But gradually we became aware that God was doing something deep in her life. She was being baptized in the Holy Spirit and she was later to speak in tongues.

From that time onwards our confidence increased, and in the course of the coming years we were to pray for hundreds of people to receive this blessing. We soon discovered they didn't have to fall down on the

17

floor. The doctrine we had come to grasp and under-stand, and which we had experienced ourselves, has been thoroughly tested in practice. In other words—it works. So it seemed sensible to write about it and so share what God was doing with a wider number of people. The first edition of this book was the result of that decision.

Once we have been baptized in the Spirit we must not stand still. There is work to do for God and much more to learn. We have found that neither denomination, nor age, nor nationality, nor race, is a barrier to receiving this experience. Joel prophesied it would happen to 'all flesh' (Joel 2:28), so that means every kind of person—children and octogenarians, Roman Catholics and Plymouth Brethren, brand new converts, in some cases while the water of their baptism is still wet on them, and experienced Christians, who have been trying to serve the Lord for many years. God means what he says.

The present world situation does not allow room for complacency. The church is too weak to play the part it could and should in the world at large. We are still far too engrossed with petty and insignificant matters. Resolutions, statements, debates and discussions will get us nowhere. We must come back cap in hand to our God and trust him to fill us with the Holy Spirit.

The contents of this book have been tested and found to be true by others. The baptism in the Holy Spirit does not provide an *easy* answer, nor is it a simple and straightforward pathway. We are ushered by it into more conflict than we have ever known before. But it does bring, to those who will trust God and obey him, joy and peace in doing God's will and the satisfaction of

18

seeing steady fruit in our lives.

A new outpouring of the Holy Spirit is essential if the church is to do God's will, and this means you. It is no good passing the buck to everyone else. Have you been filled with the Holy Spirit? Is your life characterized by freedom? Are you seeing results in your work for the Lord? Are your prayers being answered and is your church growing? Have you control over your behaviour and does it reflect the character of Christ?

As you read on, let the Holy Spirit teach you. Lay aside prejudices. Take each step as it comes, and there is no reason why you should not receive what so many believers are receiving. It may be for you the missing link in the chain of God's eternal purposes for your life. 'Ask, and it will be given you,' said Jesus, referring to the gift of the Holy Spirit (Luke 11:9). 'For *every one* who asks receives...' and you could not have it put more comprehensively than that.

2

The Missing Link

I do not wonder at what men suffer—but I wonder often at what men miss.   John Ruskin

The purpose of this book is to point very simply to something vital which you as a Christian may have missed. The New Testament church had much which we do not seem to possess. Materially we are far better off. We do not say as Peter had to—'silver and gold have I none.' We have buildings, liturgies, learning and scholarship, and many professional ministers. The early church had little of these. Its worship was largely spontaneous and extempore. It met in private homes. Its leaders were ignorant and unlearned and even the great apostle Paul earned his own living for much of the time. But spiritually there is no comparison. The early church for all its faults (and it had them) was incomparably greater in spiritual stature and more effective than most of our churches.

There was one secret they knew which we today know little about in personal experience—the Holy Spirit. Pentecost was more to them than an interesting piece of church history. It was a vivid experience which was shared by Christians and regarded as essential for the success of the church. It seems to have been more important to the life of the Christian than baptism or the Lord's Supper.

It is this secret which we have largely forgotten. A letter received from a minister pinpoints this:

> I am now 75 and just beginning to learn that the church (and we within it) has been living the wrong side of Pentecost. I fear it is too late for us to do much in our little corner of the vineyard; but we pray that even at this late hour we may be baptized with the Spirit.

Like a stream this blessing has often become lost in the sands of time. But again and again in history it has come to the surface and been rediscovered by thirsty Christian pilgrims. Samuel Chadwick, the well-known Methodist, was one such pilgrim. Early in 1882 he discovered what he called 'this fountain of living water':

> I received the gift of the Holy Spirit. I was led in ways I did not know, for I had hardly so much as heard that such an experience was possible.[3]

He goes on to relate how all this came about:

> Twelve of us began to pray in band, and the answer came ... God led us to Pentecost. The key to all my life is in that experience. It awakened my mind as well as cleansed my heart. It gave me a new joy and a new power, a new love and a new compassion. It gave me a new Bible and a new message. Above all else, it gave me a new intimacy in the communion and ministry of prayer; it taught me to pray in the Spirit.[4]

There is no *Amen* at the end of the Acts of the Apostles, and God's people can do similar exploits in the power of the same Spirit. God has not changed, nor have his promises.

It is the great privilege of the church to 'make disciples of all nations', and then to 'baptize them'. But there is a vital ministry it has either totally neglected or relegated to being a powerless ritual. Paul in Galatians 3:5 called it 'supplying the Spirit'. The nearest equivalent regularly practised by some churches is confirmation. But this has for the most part been emptied of significance; for many it is only a kind of church graduation ceremony. Andrew Murray, the South African church leader in the early part of this century, called it 'leading believers to the Holy Spirit', though to be strictly accurate it is better to see it as leading people to Jesus Christ, who is the Baptizer in the Holy Spirit. The church has neglected to lift up Christ as the Baptizer in the Spirit as well as the Lamb of God who takes away the sin of the world. Whenever this truth is taught and believed, Christians are empowered and churches begin to grow.

What is this experience?

What should we call this experience? It seems when we examine the New Testament that it had many names. Luke called it 'the promise of the Father' (Acts 1:4; cf. Lk 24:49; Acts 2:33) and Peter calls it 'the gift of the Holy Spirit' (Acts 2:38). In John and in Luke it is called 'being baptized in the Holy Spirit' (Jn 1:33; Acts 1:5; 11:16). It was also called 'receiving the Holy Spirit' (Acts 8:17; 10:47; 19:2) and 'being filled with the Holy

Spirit' (Acts 2:4; 9:17). The action of the Holy Spirit is also described in various ways, such as 'coming upon' (Lk 1:35; Acts 19:6), 'clothing' (Lk 24:49), 'falling upon' (Acts 10:44; 11:15) and 'poured out' (Acts 2:33; 10:45). If the writers of the New Testament were so diverse in their descriptions, so surely can we be. We should not be afraid of using the term 'baptism in the Holy Spirit', although normally we need to explain simply what is meant by it, as for many it will still be unfamiliar.

At this point we need to establish some basic principles in our quest for understanding what this all means.

(1) We need to grasp the importance of seeing the truth about the Holy Spirit in the Scriptures rather than either the traditions of the church or personal experience. Tradition can be important in our discovering the meaning of the Scriptures, and we would be foolish to ignore the wisdom of 2,000 years of Christianity. As we have already seen it is no good *understanding* the Scriptures if that is where it leaves us. Our understanding needs to take us on to *experiencing* the truth we have come to understand. But our traditions and experiences need to be moulded by the Scriptures, and not vice versa. We must never allow our experience, *or our lack of experience,* to judge the truth. It is just as foolish to say, 'I haven't experienced it, therefore it can't be true,' as it is to say, 'I have experienced it, therefore it must be true.'

But the Scriptures need to be interpreted correctly, and here too we need to be careful to see that the Holy Spirit is really directing us and we are not simply following the traditions of men. Some may say, 'It has always been interpreted this way,' when in effect that interpretation has been wrong in the past. Bad interpretations can be as harmful as bad traditions.

Then we need to make sure we are interpreting the whole of the Scriptures and not just our favourite portions. We need to remember that although the Acts of the Apostles is an *historical* account of what the Holy Spirit did in the early church, it is largely about the activity of the apostles, and there must have been consistency between what they believed and what they did. Indeed what the apostles *did* is vital to our understanding of what they *believed*. Apostolic action cannot contradict apostolic doctrine.

The promise we are considering in this book is based on the word of God. We must look for it in the whole of the Bible. In the next chapter we shall be seeking to discover what this promise is. We shall see the root of it in the prophets of the Old Testament, the stem or trunk in the gospels, and the flower or fruits in the Acts of the Apostles and the epistles. We must be sure that this is a divine promise which is offered to us before we can confidently receive it by faith. We have no warrant to seek for experiences which are not clearly promised us in the word of God.

(2) The second principle is that the promised blessing should be simple to understand and appropriate. For if this is a promise for all Christians regardless of their natural or spiritual maturity, then it must be simple enough for all to receive it.

In the early church the blessing was the normal accompaniment of conversion and not a compulsory second stage of spiritual experience. It was a gift received by faith, not a reward for progress in the Christian life. And most important of all—it was not a complicated doctrine, which could only be understood after years of study, but a simple promise which the youngest and most immature convert could understand and appropriate by faith.

Dr R. A. Torrey, a great Bible teacher as well as the best known evangelist of his generation, never lost sight of the essential simplicity of the Bible. Writing about this principle he said:

I am always suspicious of profound explanations of the scriptures, explanations that require a scholar or philosopher to understand them. The Bible is the plain man's book. In at least 99 times in a 100 the meaning of scripture that lies on the surface, the meaning that any simple-minded man, woman or child who really wants to know the truth and obey it would see in it, is what it really means. I have great sympathy with the little child who when she once heard a learned man attempt to explain away the plain meaning of scripture exclaimed, 'If God did not mean what He said, why didn't He say what He meant?' Well, God always does say what He means, just what you and I would understand by it if our wills were really surrendered to God, and we really desired to know exactly what God wished to tell us, and not to read our own opinions into the Bible. [5]

(3) The third principle we should follow concerns our motive—which should be the glory of God in everything. There is no justification in the New Testament for Christians seeking or expecting bizarre experiences in themselves. The Holy Spirit will only glorify Christ. Our motive in this search is all important. Dr R. A. Torrey again:

Why should we desire the baptism in the Spirit?... In order that God may be glorified in our being baptised or filled with the Holy Spirit. Because we can no longer endure it that God should be any longer dishonoured by the low level of our living, and by the ineffectiveness of our service; in order that God may be glorified by our being empowered to lead such lives as honour Him..... And when we get to praying for the baptism in the Spirit along that line it will not be many hours before we are thus baptised with the Spirit of God.[6]

The fourth principle is that our search needs to be undertaken seriously. It is no good trifling with God. If we are casual about the whole matter it is unlikely that anything will come of it. Paul warned Christians about 'quenching the Holy Spirit' (1 Thessalonians 5:19). The effectiveness and fruitfulness of our Christian life will depend on this issue, and no serious-minded Christian should dismiss the subject lightly. Much is going to depend on how we answer the question Paul addressed to the Ephesians in Acts 19:2, 'Did you receive the Holy Spirit when you believed?'

3

Seeing the Promise

We need to remember that we live in an experience-oriented age, all the way from existentialist philosophy to the drug culture and the occult. People want to feel something, not just to be told, and they are willing to explore any area in which there is something to be experienced and use any method, even drugs, to achieve it.

But I am not writing about a kind of 'Holy Spirit trip' which will induce goose pimples and make us feel good. We are to look for God's promise, *not* experiences for their own sake, and set our motivation on the right course—obedience to God and the coming of his kingdom on earth. Experiences can be deceiving. They can lead us seriously astray, and that is why we need to take the Scriptures in our hands to lead us through the modern mine-fields of emotional and psychological experience for its own sake. To say 'I feel good' is not the point.

Only if this blessing is clearly promised in the word of God can we confidently receive it and enjoy its benefits. In this chapter we are concerned to discover what this promise is—to unearth it from the soil of the Bible and see it with the eyes of faith.

Before we study this or any other subject we need to pray for understanding. One of the finest prayers for this is in Paul's letter to the Ephesians (1:17-18). Let us make it our own. Shall we pray?

> O God, give me a spirit of wisdom and of revelation in the knowledge of thee. Enlighten the eyes of my heart *that I may know.* ...

We shall never see this promise if we are shackled to the opinions of men. For George Müller this discovery was the turning point of his life. He wrote in his memoirs what God was beginning to show him:

> ... that the Word of God alone is our standard of judgment in spiritual things; that it can be explained only by the Holy Spirit and that in our day, as well as in former times, He is the teacher of His people. The result of this was that the first evening that I shut myself into my room to give myself to prayer and meditation over the Scriptures, I learned more in a few hours than I had done during a period of several months previously.... I returned to London much better in body, and as to my soul, the change was so great, that it was like a second conversion.[7]

The Bible contains many promises. But in this book we are concentrating on one of the most important—the promise of the Holy Spirit. It is plainly set forth to us as a promise in the words of Jesus (Lk 24:49; Acts 1:4-5), in the address that Peter gave on the day of Pentecost (Acts 2:33,39), and in the writings of Paul (Gal 3:14; Eph 1:13). But we need first to see the promise in some of the prophets of the Old Testament.

The Old Testament prophets

One of the most important themes of the Old Testament prophets concerned the coming of the Messiah. Some of these prophecies had a double fulfilment. They referred to the immediate future as well as the distant. Most of the prophecies concerning the Messiah could be crystallized into two main portraits—a servant and a king; he was going to suffer and he was going to be empowered. We see this clearest in the two prophecies in Isaiah 53 and 61. The Messiah was 'despised and rejected by men; a man of sorrows, and acquainted with grief' (Is 53:3) but also one upon whom the Spirit was to rest, an anointed one, 'to bring good tidings to the afflicted... to bind up the brokenhearted, to proclaim liberty to the captives' (Is 61:1).

Of course both these prophecies were fulfilled in Jesus Christ, as the New Testament indicates (see Mt 8:17 and Lk 4:18-19). But there is an interesting twist to this. In Jesus' day his contemporaries were very ready to see Jesus as the anointed servant of Yahweh proclaiming 'liberty to the captives'. They were hoping for a revolutionary—certainly not a martyr. So they easily accepted Isaiah 61, but had no place in their calculations for a suffering servant. It is no wonder that when their Messiah did come they not only failed to recognize him, but actively contributed to his unjust condemnation and execution.

But today we face a quite different situation. The church is all too ready to accept the image of the suffering Christ, the crucified Messiah, but is strangely reluctant to see him as the conquering king, miraculously delivering people from disease and death and freeing them from the power of Satan. The balance has been upset and the church more often appears as a defeated community than a triumphant body of people endued with the power of the Holy Spirit and manifesting the same signs and wonders which Jesus did. We have gone to the other extreme.

The prophets not only saw the coming of the Messiah but also the inauguration of the new covenant between God and his people. Jeremiah wrote, 'Behold, the days are coming... when I will make a new covenant with the house of Israel and the house of Judah' (Jer 31:31). Ezekiel declared that the new covenant would include not only cleansing from sins, but the gift of a new heart and a new spirit. 'I will sprinkle clean water upon you, and you shall be clean from all your uncleannesses, and from all your idols I will cleanse you. A new heart I will give you, and a new spirit I will put within you; and I will take out of your flesh the heart of stone and give you a heart of flesh. And I will put my spirit within you, and cause you to walk in my statutes and be careful to observe my ordinances' (Ezek 36:25-27). The gift of the Spirit is thus linked with the promise of forgiveness and cleansing.

But the clearest and most dramatic description of this blessing is seen in the prophecy of Joel. 'And it shall come to pass afterward, that I will pour out my spirit on all flesh; your sons and your daughters shall prophesy, your old men shall dream dreams and your young men shall see visions. Even upon the menservants and maidservants in those days, I will pour out my Spirit' (Joel 2:28-29). Here is the promise of a profusion of spiritual power and manifestations.

So the Old Testament prophets saw the coming of the

Messiah as the one who would inaugurate the new covenant or agreement with his people, which was to be sealed by the blood of Christ for the cleansing of our sins, and who would also bestow his Spirit on his people to empower them to do his will in the world.

John the Baptist

John the Baptist was a 'bridge' prophet who belonged in a sense to both the old and the new covenants. Jesus described him as 'the greatest' of the Old Testament prophets, which was the highest compliment he could possibly have paid to his cousin (Lk 7:28). John was given the difficult role of linking the old with the new, of bridging a generation gap and of introducing Jesus Christ to the public.

This introduction took place beside the River Jordan where John was baptizing people. Suddenly he saw Jesus advancing towards him. As he approached, John pointed to him and said, 'Behold, the Lamb of God, who takes away the sin of the world . . . this is he who baptizes with the Holy Spirit . . . this is the Son of God' (Jn 1:29,33,34). I have deliberately picked out those phrases which John the Baptist used to express his beliefs about the One for whom he was preparing the way. Jesus is declared to be the Lamb of God, the Baptizer in the Holy Spirit and the Son of God. Most Christians know Christ as the Saviour and the Son—but in many churches Jesus has never been lifted up as the Baptizer in the Holy Spirit. It is important to notice that it was God himself who revealed to John that he was to call him the Baptizer; as he had baptized people in the river Jordan, so Jesus would in the Holy Spirit. And

Jesus himself, as we shall see, accepted this designation as the Baptizer. So John brought into clearer perspective the dual ministry of Jesus, which had been foreseen years before by the prophets of the Old Testament, particularly Isaiah.

We see these truths also in Paul's letter to the Galatians (4:4-6)—

(1) *The coming of the Son*—'when the time had fully come, God sent forth his Son'.

(2) *The salvation he came to bring*—'to redeem those who were under the law'.

(3) *The coming of the Spirit*—'And because you are sons, God has sent the Spirit of his Son into our hearts, crying, "Abba! Father!" '

It is most important to recognize that the source of power is not in an experience but in Jesus Christ himself. It is not in the gift, but in the Giver. Jesus said, 'If any one thirst, *let him come to me*.' We first come to Jesus with the sin problem, but we also come to Him with the problem of powerlessness. This baptism is his prerogative, and he is the only Spirit-baptizer. On the day of Pentecost it was Jesus who poured out what the crowd saw and heard, and baptized them with the Holy Spirit; and it is Jesus who has officiated ever since in its administration. Men and women may be links in the chain that brings us into this great belssing, but the Lord Jesus Christ is the One from whom we receive it. If we already know him as Lord, it should be easy for us to come to him for this gift also.

Jesus Christ

When Jesus came to John the Baptist for baptism, the humble prophet at first refused. 'I need to be baptized

32

by you,' he said. Jesus replied, 'Let it be so now; for thus it is fitting for us to fulfil all righteousness' (Mt 3:14-15). Then John consented.

Jesus had no sins to confess. But he knew that he had been called to be 'like his brethren in every respect' (Heb 2:17). Levertoff comments, 'In undergoing baptism Jesus is accepting His destiny.'[8] Jesus' destiny was twofold—to be made sin for us, and to pour out the Holy Spirit upon us. So he went down into Jordan for baptism, and coming out of the water received the power of the Holy Spirit for his ministry.

Being like us in every respect means that he identified himself completely with us. He was truly and fully human. The only difference was that he never sinned. He was the second Adam, thus restoring man to the perfect humanity which the first Adam forfeited for us. Being like us in every other aspect he needed the power of the Holy Spirit to do the will of God, in the same sense that we do.

It is important for us to understand that Jesus, though born of the Spirit and living a perfect life in the Spirit, still received as an additional blessing the anointing of the same Spirit for his three years' ministry. Jesus did no miracles, gave no teaching and made no mark on society until he had been 'anointed with the Holy Spirit and with power' (Acts 10:38). Then the impact of his life and ministry was immediate and striking. We are told 'Jesus returned in the power of the Spirit into Galilee, and a report concerning him went out through all the surrounding country. And he taught in their synagogues, being glorified by all' (Lk 4:14-15). On his first visit to his home and the synagogue where he had worshipped for so long, he did nothing more spectacular than read a lesson. But when he sat down he found 'the eyes of all in the synagogue were fixed on him' (Lk 4:20).

F. B. Meyer, the great Baptist preacher and Keswick speaker of the start of this century, has put it well:

Jesus Christ was conceived of the Holy Ghost, and for thirty years was led and taught by the divine Spirit. Was He not one with the Holy Spirit? Certainly. Why then must He be anointed? Because His human nature needed to be empowered by the Spirit before even He could do successful service in this world. Jesus waited for thirty years until He was anointed, and only then did He say, 'The Spirit of the Lord is upon me, and He hath anointed me to preach.' Never forget that our Lord's ministry was not in the power of the second person of the blessed Trinity, but in the power of the third person.[9]

This should cause us to examine our lives carefully. Have we been born of the Spirit? If so—have we been baptized in the Spirit? Dr A. B. Simpson challenges us along the same lines:

First, Christ was born of the Spirit, then He was baptised by the Spirit, and then He went forth to work out His life and ministry in the power of the Spirit. But 'He that sanctifieth and they that are sanctified are all of one'; so in like manner we must follow in His footsteps and re-live our life. Born like Him of the Spirit, we must be baptised of the Spirit, and then go forth to live His life and reproduce His work.[10]

It might be right here to consider how this promise relates to us. A Christian is one who has been born of

34

the Spirit, or born from above, as Jesus explained to Nicodemus (Jn 3:3). The authority to be called the sons of God comes only to those who have received Christ and been born of God (Jn 1:12-13). This too is a neglected truth in the church today. But the promise we are considering is not directly related to our birth into the family of God through the operation of the Holy Spirit, but our receiving power through the same Holy Spirit to function properly in the body of Christ. The church on the day of Pentecost was already born of the Spirit. This may either have taken place in the upper room on the first Easter evening (Jn 20:22) or more likely earlier still on the grounds of their faith in Christ. Jesus told them that their names had been written in heaven (Lk 10:20) and that they were already clean (Jn 13:10-11). But on that day the church was baptized in the Spirit. Just as the sacred body of the Saviour was born of the Spirit and thirty years later baptized in the Spirit, so the church as the body of Christ on earth was first born of the Spirit and then endued with the power of the Spirit. Jesus' teaching about being born of the Spirit was nothing new. Indeed he rebuked Nicodemus for not knowing about it. 'Are you a teacher of Israel, and yet you do not understand this?' (Jn 3:10), he said to this ruler of the Jews. But the promise we are considering is something new and different from re-generation. The promise is never stated in terms of 'life', but always of 'power'. Jesus promised his disciples 'power' when the Holy Spirit came upon them (Lk 24:49; Acts 1:8). The confusion between the work of the Spirit in regeneration—the sign of which is baptism —and his work in bestowing power, is one of the main hindrances to people seeing the promise and receiving it. R. A. Torrey has put it well:

> A man may be regenerated by the Holy Spirit, and still not be baptized with the Holy Spirit. In regeneration, there is the impartation of life by the Spirit's power, and the one who receives it is saved: in the baptism with the Holy Spirit, there is the impartation of power and the one who receives it is fitted for service.[11]

All this as we have seen was exemplified in the life of Christ. But it was strikingly portrayed also in his teaching. Jesus was indeed a teacher sent from God. Like the wise steward in his own parable he gave his disciples their food 'at the proper time' (Mt 24:45). He taught them progressively. There were matters which had to be left until after the coming of the Holy Spirit. 'You cannot bear them now,' he said to them (Jn 16:12). It was towards the end of his ministry that Jesus taught most about the Holy Spirit and what he would do when he came.

But there are some interesting references to the Holy Spirit in his earlier sayings. In John 7:38 he likens the blessing which the coming of the Holy Spirit would bring to 'rivers of living water' flowing out from the believer. And in Luke 11:13 he speaks of the Father giving the Holy Spirit to those who ask. This reference is crucial. Christ could not have meant this promise for unbelievers, for they could not receive (Jn 14:17) and would not ask. Literally Christ said that the Holy Spirit would be given to 'those who *go on asking*'. If Christians receive automatically at conversion—then why go on asking? No promise of Scripture is ever received automatically. It is 'through faith and patience' that we inherit God's promises (Heb 6:12). But it was at the Last Supper that Jesus told them that the Spirit had been with them, but would then be in them (Jn 14:17); that he would teach them all things and remind them of his words (Jn 14:26); that he would bear witness to him (Jn 15:26); that he would convince the world of sin, righteousness and judgement (Jn 16:8) and guide them into all truth (Jn 16:13). Above all, he would glorify Christ (Jn 16:14).

But the phrase that comes prominently is 'when he comes'. The disciples must have wondered when this would be. They knew that it would be after Jesus had ascended. But after his resurrection he made it clear to them that the coming of the Holy Spirit was imminent. 'Behold, I send the promise of my Father upon you; but stay in the city, until you are clothed with power from on high' (Lk 24:49). And later 'he charged them not to depart from Jerusalem, but to wait for the promise of the Father, which, he said, "you heard from me, for John baptized with water, but before many days you shall be baptized with the Holy Spirit"' (Acts 1:4-5).

So the circle is completed. The same Jesus who was declared to be the Baptizer in the Holy Spirit beside the river Jordan, takes the same expression on his lips to describe what he was about to do for his disciples, and for succeeding generations of believers who would receive the same promise by faith.

The promise has now crystallized into one simple statement—the promise of the Father. For it is the Father from whom the promise comes, it is the Son through whom it comes, and it is the Holy Spirit who is the promise itself.

The chief concomitant of the promise is 'power'. 'You

shall receive *power* when the Holy Spirit has come upon you' (Acts 1:8). As we have seen, he also described the promise as being 'clothed with power from on high' (Lk 24:49). James Denney has written: 'Anyone who wishes to know the New Testament connotation of Spirit must use his concordance also for the term "power" which is its chief content.'

But we may add to this general promise of power the other effects that the coming of the Holy Spirit will have upon Christians. Jesus said that their hearts would become like 'rivers of living water'. He said that through them the world would be convinced of sin, righteousness and judgement. He said that they would be led into all truth.

So much then for this great promise. I trust that the Holy Spirit has shown it to us and we are beginning to desire earnestly 'the promise of the Father'. R. W. Dale has written:

> The ancient promises are unrecalled. By earnest prayer we may obtain from Christ the gift of the Spirit, as we trust we have already obtained the remission of sins. [12]

In the next chapter we hope to show how this great promise may be received by every child of God in a greater measure than at the time of conversion.

4

Receiving the Promise

By now we should have become aware of the fact that
there is a promise of power in the Scriptures for all
Christian people. Next we need to find out how we can
receive it, how we can experience it in our lives.
Whereas the Old Testament prophets 'saw it from
afar', and few of them ever received it, we can have the
joy of entering into all they saw, and much more.

We need to make sure we do not fail to enter because
of unbelief. Jesus is the Joshua of the New Testament,
leading the people of God into their rich inheritance. He
came as the Lamb of God to take away our sins, and as
the Baptizer in the Holy Spirit to endue us with power
for his service. Both blessings are our birthright, and
from Pentecost onwards have been available from
him—and can be received by faith.

In this chapter the main question which we have to
answer is: how does a Christian receive the promised
baptism in the Holy Spirit? But first we must try to
answer: to whom is this promise made and when do we
receive it? The natural place for us to turn to for the
answers is the Acts of the Apostles, because here we
see in the opening chapter of the church's history how

the earliest Christians received this blessing.

There are some people who question the use of such evidence upon which to build anything definite. It is true that we should not look for the promise itself in the Acts, but we are surely justified in learning from the manner in which the blessing was received by those who were nearest in time to the first proclamation of the promise and who knew Jesus in the flesh. After all, it is part of the New Testament! In it we see apostolic doctrine in action. In essence it is a book about 'acts'—it shows us what the apostles *did* as well as what they *taught*. It would be wrong for us to look for the complete doctrine of the Holy Spirit in Acts, but we can find out how the apostles understood this doctrine and acted upon it. One of the most reliable canons of biblical interpretation is to observe how the original hearers understood doctrine—otherwise we are always in danger of imposing on our interpretation pre-suppositions of our own. In the Acts, therefore, we should be able to discover how the apostles thought the promise of the Holy Spirit was to be received. The actions of the apostles, in other words, indicate how they understood their doctrine. When, therefore, we discover that such illustrious apostles as Peter, John and Paul laid hands on believers *after* they had been baptized in water in order that they might receive the baptism in the Holy Spirit, we know that they could not have believed in a doctrine which taught that this blessing was *automatically* received at the moment of conversion and baptism.

But there is an even more important point to consider. The Acts of the Apostles is often and rightly called the Acts of the Holy Spirit. In this book we read not only about what the apostles did but also the Holy Spirit. We might be bold enough to say that the apostles were wrong in their actions and misapplied their doctrine of the Spirit, but it would be a brazen person indeed who would dare to say that the Holy Spirit himself acted contrary to the doctrine concerning his person and work. Thus we see in Acts that when the apostles prayed for the Christians at Samaria that they might receive the baptism in the Holy Spirit, he came to them when hands were applied (Acts 8:17). So too in Acts 19 the Holy Spirit responded to the faith of Paul and the twelve at Ephesus (Acts 19:6). We must be very careful not to bind the activity of the Holy Spirit with an inadequate doctrine of his work.

The famous passages in Acts which tell us of the activity of the Holy Spirit in relation to the believer are vital in our quest to discover how and when we may receive the gift of the Holy Spirit. There are six occasions in all—not counting the occasion when Christians who had already received the promised Holy Spirit were freshly anointed with the same Spirit when in prayer together (Acts 4:31). But we are only concerned in this chapter with the initial receiving of this blessing.

The day of Pentecost (Acts 2:1-42)

Here we have two occasions which we should take together—for two groups of people received the promised Holy Spirit on the same day. First the church, and then a crowd of three thousand which had gathered at the sound of the church speaking in tongues for the first time.

There is a quick and easy answer to the question, 'Who is eligible for the promise?' In the Acts of the Apostles *all* who are open and seriously seeking this blessing receive it. No one gets left out. When the Holy Spirit came at Pentecost and Jesus baptized the church in his power, we are told that *all* were filled with the Holy Spirit and spoke in tongues, men and women (including the Virgin Mary who was present), apostles and lay people. A little bit later when Peter addressed the crowd which gathered to ask questions, he told them that the promise was not only for them but also for the Gentiles and indeed anyone who would fulfil the simple and straightforward conditions of repentance and baptism, for in these last days God was pouring out his Spirit on all flesh.

The second question is also simple to answer—when can the promise be received? If Peter had said 'repent *and believe* and you shall receive the gift of the Holy Spirit', then it could reasonably be argued that this gift is received the moment a person believes in Christ. But Peter said 'repent and *be baptized*', which is different. Of course, Christian baptism presupposes faith in Christ, but the enquirers at Pentecost would have clearly understood what Peter meant by these words, namely that they would neither receive the forgiveness of sins nor the same experience as the 120, i.e. the baptism in the Spirit, until they had repented and been baptized in the name of Jesus Christ. Repentance and faith would have needed to be seen to be real before the early church would have baptized anyone. But the point that is being made is that baptism takes time, whereas faith is instantaneous; therefore, Peter's words imply that some passage of time normally would elapse between water baptism and receiving the baptism in the Spirit.

Samaria (Acts 8:4-24)

The expansion of the church seems at first to have been slow geographically. The church took Jesus at his word—*first* in Jerusalem*—and the home church seems to have grown very fast in those early years. No doubt the men and women baptized in water and in the Spirit at Pentecost would have trickled back to the countries from which they had travelled, taking the gospel with them. But it was a fierce persecution that suddenly scattered the large church in Jerusalem—and they began to spread the good news around Judea and Samaria.

An evangelist called Philip came to a city of Samaria and preached Christ to the people. Many believed and were baptized. But for some reason or other they did not receive the baptism in the Holy Spirit. Samaritans were exceptionally legalistic in religious background—they did not accept the inspiration of the Old Testament prophets—so this may have accounted for their slowness to respond to the moving of the Holy Spirit.

There is a very interesting question which needs answering in connection with this story. How did anyone know that the Samaritans had not received the baptism in the Holy Spirit when they believed and were baptized in water? We are told that there was much joy in the city (Acts 8:8), but this does not seem to have been taken as a sign. The only possible explanation is to be found in the absence of supernatural manifestations.

An interesting conclusion can be drawn from this. Since Pentecost there had been many conversions, and the converts had received the Spirit. In every case there must have been supernatural manifestations, or the Samaritan position would not have struck anyone as an exception. No one seems to have said, 'Perhaps these believers have received the baptism in the Spirit quietly

43

and unconsciously." There may well have been a reason other than the legalistic background of the Samaritans for their delay in receiving the gift of the Holy Spirit. The view which has often been advanced may be valid— namely that the delay was in order that the unity of the church might be kept and that the Jewish apostles might be the means of blessing to the Samaritans.

At all events the news got through to Jerusalem, and Peter and John were sent off to investigate. First they prayed, and then they laid hands on them, and they received the baptism in the Holy Spirit. We know too that there was nothing vague about their reception of this blessing, for a magician, Simon Magus, who was standing by *saw* the Spirit given. Something very definite must have happened to them, for the magician tried to buy this power with money.

Here too we have the answers to our questions. Other scriptures bear witness to the truth that the Holy Spirit indwells every true believer at the moment of his conversion; thus we realize that the indwelling Holy Spirit was given to all those who had first believed and been baptized, except Simon Magus. Also, on the day of Pentecost the three thousand probably received the baptism in the Spirit shortly after they were baptized; here there was a longer delay, and they received some time afterward through the ministry of Peter and John.

Paul (Acts 9:1-19)

Paul's conversion took place suddenly outside Damascus and yet there were years of preparation before his encounter with Jesus. We know of one incident in that preparation because Luke tells us that Saul, as he was then called, was present at the assassination of Stephen and would have heard his cries, 'Lord, do not hold this sin against them' (Acts 7:60). Paul was struck blind at the moment when Christ appeared to him and so had to be led by his travelling companions into the city of Damascus. For the next three days, crippled by his blindness, he fasted and prayed. Then God sent a rather reluctant layman called Ananias, who had been reassured by God that Paul had an important future role to play in the church, that he might 'regain [his] sight and be filled with the Holy Spirit' (Acts 9:17). There was an immediate response; he was healed when 'something like scales fell from his eyes', and presumably he *was* then filled with the Holy Spirit. He was immediately baptized in water and broke his fast.

There are a number of interesting factors in this story. In the first place, God sent a layman to minister to Paul. There is a greater need than ever today to see the emancipation of the laity from the shackles that many churches have put upon them. Not only is the blessing of the baptism in the Spirit intended for laity as well as ministers, but the laity are just as capable of bringing people into this experience—and, of course, healing also—as ministers are. It never has been intended for ministers only.

Another interesting feature of this story is the order in which Ananias ministered. Paul was already converted and had presumably repented. His healing came first, and only later his baptism. We are not told when Paul was 'filled with the Holy Spirit'; it could have been before, during or after his baptism in water. The order of events was never regarded as important in the New Testament and the order varies from story to story. But what was important was that Christian initiation included being filled with the Holy Spirit as well as being baptized in water.

Cornelius and his household (Acts 10:1-48)

We now move to Caesarea, where a godfearing Roman officer called Cornelius was stationed. Although not yet a baptized Christian, the Holy Spirit was clearly at work in his life. He was a man of prayer and generous in his giving. Cornelius had a vision telling him to send for Peter who was staying at Joppa at the time. Peter meanwhile had also received instructions from the Holy Spirit and a special vision to prepare his prejudiced mind to preach to Gentiles. Cornelius invited his relations and friends to his house and Peter addressed them.

In the middle of his talk about Christ, the Holy Spirit came on all those who were listening in exactly the same manner as he had come on the day of Pentecost. This convinced Peter and his companions that they should go ahead and baptize them at once, for clearly these Gentiles had received the Holy Spirit in the same way as they themselves had on the day of Pentecost.

So again we need to notice that *all of them* received the blessing, and in this case it took place actually as they were listening to Peter's address and not through the ministry of the laying-on of hands. It was a spontaneous experience. We need always to be open to the surprises of the Holy Spirit. God often blesses unlikely people in unlikely situations, and it is not for us to judge or question what God does. When Peter reported to the church in Jerusalem what had happened to these Gentiles, the church was quite clear that Peter had acted correctly. Obviously this had been a divine intervention and could very well happen again. It is interesting also to note in passing that Peter used the expression 'to be baptized in the Spirit' in his report, clear evidence that the term was being used years after the day of Pentecost (Acts 11:16).

This story should be a warning to all those Christians who, in their efforts to tidy up the teaching in the New Testament, imprison the Holy Spirit in doctrinal systems, almost forbidding him to work outside them. But the Holy Spirit will not be tied down in this way. Any doctrinal formulation which has the action of the Holy Spirit cut and dried, and does not make allowances for these 'surprises', will hinder God's people from being used and will quench the Holy Spirit. The New Testament reveals a multiplicity of ways in which the Holy Spirit works, and we need to take our hands off and let him work the way he wants to. He only requires our obedience and co-operation and a willingness to allow our prejudices to be laid aside, as Peter was prepared to do in the home of Cornelius.

Ephesus (Acts 19:1-7)

The next story short-circuits all the neat reconstructions of men when they attempt to show a consistent pattern in the Acts stories. There are some people who point to the stories of the Samaritans and Cornelius and say they were exceptional—we might call them Samaritan and Gentile Pentecosts. But there are many who, in attempting to tidy up the Acts narratives, find this story almost impossible to fit into neat categories.

The incident took place some twenty years after the day of Pentecost. Paul on this his first visit to Ephesus found twelve disciples. Something about them puzzled the apostle so he asked them the leading question, 'Did you receive the Holy Spirit when you believed?' They replied that they had not even heard of the Holy Spirit.

Now we do not know whether these disciples were true believers or not. They were certainly very ignorant of basic Christian doctrine and deficient in elementary spiritual experience. All we do know is that Paul systematically corrected them. They had been baptized into John's baptism, so he told them about Jesus, whom John told men to believe in. He administered Christian baptism. And then as a quite separate procedure he laid his hands on them, and the Holy Spirit came on them as twenty years before upon the church at Pentecost.

The vital thing to notice about this story is that it really does not matter what the spiritual condition of these disciples *had been* before Paul ministered to them. Whether they were true Christians or not we shall never know for certain; but it does not matter one way or the other. They certainly must have been by the time Paul baptized them. And the crucial point is that Paul did not simply walk away from them after he had baptized them. He did not say to them, 'Now you have been baptized you have got everything.' But instead he ministered the baptism of the Spirit to them. He laid hands on them. And his prayers were instantly answered with practical and tangible results—they 'spoke with tongues and prophesied'. There is no way anyone can get out of the implications of this story. It is one of our mandates for praying for Christians (with or without the laying-on of hands) to be filled with the Holy Spirit. If

Paul did, so can we. It is no good arguing from Paul's teaching in his epistles that every Christian has been baptized in the Holy Spirit. Paul would not have believed one thing and done something else that was inconsistent with it. We need to understand Paul's teaching *in the light of what he did in the Acts.*

Again we need to notice that all those whom Paul prayed for were blessed; there were no exceptions. They all received, and quite clearly it was a separate ministry from that of water baptism, though obviously connected and related.

The question Paul asked them is most revealing to our study. This question however can only mean, "Did you receive *the baptism* in the Holy Spirit when you believed?" Some might feel we are taking liberties with the text. We would respond by saying that Paul was *not* ignorant of the doctrine of the Spirit's indwelling ministry at conversion. After all, he propounded it! If he thought they believed, by virtue of his own doctrinal knowledge, he also would have known that the Holy Spirit presently indwelt them, hence no need to ask the question in the first place. Secondly, it proves that it is possible to receive the baptism in the Holy Spirit when you believe. But thirdly, it was equally clearly proven that you do not always receive it when you believe, otherwise there would have been no point in Paul asking the question. It also proves that this must have been regarded by the early church as a definitely discernible experience—for Paul expected (and received) a definite answer to his question.

Summary of the evidence

At first sight these six cases present some variation. Can we discern from them any pattern for receiving the promise of the Holy Spirit? Is there a 'normal Christian experience'?

49

The plain answer is, I suppose, no. There is no stereotype. But if we examine these incidents there are things we can learn.

We see in the Acts that Christian initiation, far from being one sacramental action, namely water baptism, was in fact a whole constellation of actions, some from God's side and some from ours. God is always the initiator. He always comes first. He sets initiation going. But in addition to God's primary move towards us, there is the part the word plays, our response of repentance and faith, water baptism, Spirit baptism (with or without the laying-on of hands, for Scripture allows both), and the manifestation of spiritual gifts. All these various parts are important, but in the way in which they interrelate, and the order in which they come, there is little in the way of a set pattern.

There is always a danger in oversimplifying the activity of the Holy Spirit. But I believe it is possible to establish some norms and detect the principles upon which the apostles worked and the Holy Spirit operated.

The norm, if there is one, was expressed by Peter on the day of Pentecost when he said, 'Repent, and be baptized every one of you in the name of Jesus Christ for the forgiveness of your sins; and you shall receive the gift of the Holy Spirit' (Acts 2:38). Normally a new convert would repent and be baptized and receive the gift of the Holy Spirit all together. But as the ministry of the apostles and the activity of the Spirit show, the order in which these were carried out and the interval of time elapsing between them was not always the same.

For instance, in Acts 8 the Samaritans believed and were baptized, but there was a delay before they received the baptism in the Holy Spirit. In Acts 9 there was a similar delay between Paul's conversion and his being filled with the Holy Spirit through the ministry of Ananias. In Acts 10 the baptism in the Holy Spirit was given before Cornelius and his friends had been baptized in water. Indeed it is not until we come to the case of the Ephesian disciples that the norm re-asserts itself. Here also the receiving of the Holy Spirit comes *after* their baptism in water (Acts 19:5-6).

Can we summarize all this into something coherent? Professor F. F. Bruce has written, 'The idea of an unbaptized Christian is simply not entertained in the New Testament.'[13] We ought to add—neither is the idea of a Christian who has not received the baptism in the Holy Spirit. In those early days Christians were deemed ready for both baptism in water and the blessing of the Spirit after they had believed. If they did not receive the Holy Spirit there and then, steps were immediately taken to pray for them and lead them into this blessing. It was a clear promise and a definite and consciously realized experience. Paul expected a clear answer to his question, 'Did you receive the Holy Spirit when you believed?' Peter and John seem to have known definitely that the Samaritans had not yet received this promise, and there was nothing vague about its reception. It seems as if the laying-on of hands was normally used when the Spirit was not spontaneously given on believing. It seems to have been the scriptural way of bestowing what may otherwise have been missed in initiation.

Other views

An absence of clear teaching is robbing many of God's people of this great promise. There are three main views which differ from the one above, but which do not accord with the evidence of the Acts of the Apostles.

The first is the view that every Christian receives the baptism in the Spirit at his conversion when he believes in Christ. He may never have even heard of the Holy Spirit, but when he is born of the Spirit he is also baptized in the Spirit. Such teaching stresses the need for an increasing 'filling' with the Spirit but not a definite receiving of the gift of the Holy Spirit subsequent to conversion. Whatever may be said for this view in other respects, it falls down on the evidence which we have in the Acts of the Apostles. Of the six incidents, in only two was the baptism in the Holy Spirit given at the moment of conversion, namely in the house of Cornelius and to the seekers at Pentecost. Even on these occasions one wonders whether a strong case can be built on them. We do not know the exact spiritual condition of the friends of Cornelius. If the others were like Cornelius then they could well have been regenerate, at least in the Old Testament sense. In the case of Pentecost there is an indication in what Peter said that baptism in water and the receiving of the Spirit were two parts of the same package rather than identical actions of God. It is possible that the baptism in the Holy Spirit was received spontaneously at the moment of baptism, but we are not told that this happened. It is equally possible that something happened as in Ephesus (Acts 19)—namely that after baptism there was the laying-on of hands for the receiving of the Holy Spirit. But we don't know for certain either way; we are only told that they were baptized (2:41).

The second view is that the baptism in the Holy Spirit is given at water baptism, or later at confirmation. This again does not fit the facts. In Acts 8 and 19 Holy Spirit baptism was given *after* water baptism as a quite distinct operation. In Acts 10 he was given *before* water baptism.

The third view is one that seems to confuse the baptism in the Spirit with sanctification. It is true that repentance is a condition for receiving this promise from God, but there is no suggestion that this blessing was promised on condition of a holy life, nor will its immediate result be a state of entire sanctification. The blessing is connected in Scripture with justification rather than sanctification. This blessing is a free gift of God—offered to all his children and able to be received by faith alone. Acts 15:8-9 is sometimes quoted in support of the view that this experience is primarily one of sanctification. But if we examine the context we shall see that it is better interpreted by taking 'cleansed' in the ritual sense of being set apart for God. Peter almost certainly had in mind his dream when God revealed to him what was clean and unclean. In other words Peter is referring to the justification rather than the sanctification of Cornelius and his friends.

The view that seems to take cognizance of all the facts of the passages we have been looking at, is that the baptism in the Spirit is a blessing received from Christ the Baptizer. It is promised to every believer and may be received by faith from the moment of conversion onwards. It may precede or follow baptism, and is a clearly discernible experience so that every Christian should be able to answer definitely the question, 'Did you receive the Holy Spirit when you believed?' In the New Testament it was part of normal Christian initiation, and primarily given that Christians might have supernatural power.

The sign of receiving

We must now turn to a controversial aspect of this experience, and perhaps the question that is asked more than any other—namely, 'What about the gift of tongues?' Do we have to speak in tongues to be baptized in the Spirit? Is speaking in tongues the initial evidence of this experience, or will another gift suffice?

Whatever may be the answer to these questions, there *is* an important part for signs to play, according to the Bible. Of the six stories we have referred to, in three of them everyone present spoke in tongues. It is not clear in Acts 19 whether they all spoke in tongues *and* prophesied or spoke in tongues *or* prophesied. Otherwise it seems to have been given to everyone at Pentecost and in the house of Cornelius.

Signs abound in the Scriptures, and they are usually physical. Under the old covenant God gave the sign of circumcision; under the new baptism in water. It is only to insincere hypocrites that the Lord usually denies signs. Jesus told his disciples that if they believed, certain signs·would follow as a confirmation of the word, and one of these is 'speaking in tongues' (Mk 16:17). This sign seems to have been in the early church the normal accompaniment of receiving the gift of the Holy Spirit, and in this sense can correctly be called the sign of this blessing.

The evidence for this can be found in the passages in the Acts which we have just considered. Let us look again more closely at the instances in the Acts when Christian initiation is specifically mentioned.

At Pentecost (the disciples), in the house of Cornelius (the Gentiles) and at Ephesus (the disciples of John the

Baptist) there is a clear statement about speaking in tongues at the moment of reception. In the case of the Samaritans it is almost certain that they did, although it is not specifically mentioned. It is clear that when Peter and John laid their hands on the Samaritan Christians something dramatic happened—so striking and unusual that Simon the magician, who had for years amazed the Samaritans with his magic and had also seen miracles and exorcism under Philip's ministry, wanted to buy it. (An alternative Greek manuscript has *theasamenos* in Acts 8:18, which is much stronger than *idōn* and suggests that Simon's eyes, speaking proverbially, popped out of his head.) Professor F. F. Bruce says,

> The context leaves us in no doubt that their reception of the Spirit was attended by external manifestations such as had marked His descent on the earliest disciples at Pentecost.[14]

Most unbiased observers would agree that it is almost certain that they spoke in tongues as they received the Holy Spirit.

In the two other cases where we are not told how they received the Holy Spirit, we cannot argue one way or the other. But in the case of Paul we know that he spoke in tongues from what he says in 1 Corinthians 14:18, although we are not told when he began to practise this gift.

It would be unwise to dogmatize on this evidence—but it is a good deal stronger than many people realize. If not conclusive, it is very compelling evidence that in the early church speaking in tongues normally accompanied the receiving of the Holy Spirit.

There are those who say that the fruit of the Spirit should be the evidence. An increase in such fruit should certainly be a result of this blessing. The transformation of the disciples from Pentecost onwards can be seen in a variety of striking ways. But it still holds true that at the moment they were filled with the Holy Spirit their response was to begin to speak in tongues 'as the Spirit gave them utterance' (Acts 2:4). Again it is of importance to notice that when the Holy Spirit fell on the household of Cornelius their response was to speak in tongues and extol God, and it was this alone that convicted the believers who came with Peter that the gift of the Holy Spirit had been poured out even upon despised Gentiles. (Compare Acts 11:17 with 10:46.)

Many people ask the question, 'Must I speak in tongues when I am baptized in the Holy Spirit?' I would suggest that it is the wrong kind of question to ask. The answer is clearly—no. God will not make us speak in tongues if we are unwilling to do so. Speaking in tongues—as indeed every activity of the Holy Spirit— requires the active co-operation of the believer. God will never make us do anything if we are unwilling to co-operate with him. The question probably implies that the person does not want to speak in tongues. A better question to ask is, 'Can I speak in tongues when I am baptized in the Holy Spirit?' The answer to this question is gloriously—yes. Speaking in tongues is described by the apostle Paul (in 1 Cor 14:2,4,15-16,22) as speaking to God, uttering mysteries in the Spirit, edifying oneself, praying with the spirit, singing with the spirit (when the Spirit inspires the melody), blessing with the spirit (giving thanks), and a sign to unbelievers. Such a wonderful list of purposes should encourage every Christian to want to speak in tongues. No wonder Paul said, 'I want you all to speak in tongues' (14:5). No wonder he writes that to forbid speaking in tongues is to disobey the command of the Lord and such a person is not to be recognized (14:37-39). It is an interesting reflection that in recent times it has sometimes been those who *have* spoken in tongues in the churches who have not been recognized.

A further question which is even more often asked is, 'Can I receive the promise of the Father, the baptism in the Spirit, without speaking in tongues?' The answer is that it is possible to receive this blessing and not *at the same time* speak in tongues. In the early church it seems to have been the normal accompaniment of the receiving of the Holy Spirit. But there are factors in our day that were not present then and which obscure the matter for us. I refer particularly to ignorance, fear and prejudice. Plainly some know little or nothing about it, and others are afraid at the very thought of it, perhaps because they think they are going to be 'taken over'. Prejudice can also be a barrier. Some have only heard negative things about it, and so have been brought up to reject it. Sometimes it is the very phrase that people object to. It might be better if we used a literal translation—'to speak in other languages'. That threatens no one.

We need to remember that in the early church speaking in tongues was a well-known gift. We call it a phenomenon, Paul didn't. In 1 Corinthians there is no indication as he writes about this gift that he is handling anything unusual. Jesus had taught his disciples about it before his ascension. There was none of that fear that seems to cripple so many Christians when they think about this subject. The early Christians had faith in the Holy Spirit and his discretion in the matter. Neither was there any prejudice—but rather Christians thanked God, as Paul did, for the benefit that this gift brought to them. Many of the early Christians were simple-minded people, ignorant and unlearned, for God chooses the foolish and the weak, the low and the despised in this world, and these people would have been more than grateful for a gift which, by-passing the mind, helped them to speak to God in the Spirit and worship and adore their Lord and Saviour in words they could never find. But it was not only the unlearned who were thankful, for the apostle Paul—a university graduate who had studied under one of the best teachers of his day—wrote years after his conversion, 'I thank God that I speak [I continue regularly to speak] in tongues more than you all' (1 Cor 14:18). In his private devotions he seems to have poured out his heart in prayer in tongues—but he is swift to add that in public he would rather speak intelligibly so that the church might be edified. Have we got further than Paul in the life of the Spirit that we do not need this aid to prayer?

Alas, today this subject is beset with much ignorance, fear and prejudice, and we need to allow the Holy Spirit to set us free from these so that he can enable us to speak in tongues. Thus there may be a time lag between our receiving the blessing and our speaking in tongues.

Another hindrance may be self-consciousness. Many a person receives this blessing at a public meeting where they may be too shy to speak in tongues in the presence of others. Often, as they go home, or when they reach the privacy of their bedrooms, they begin to praise God in this new language. We have known people receive just as in Cornelius' house—as the word is being preached. It would have been most distracting if they had begun immediately to speak in tongues, and so they have waited until the meeting was over. Apparently the friends of Cornelius were not as inhibited as many of us are, and did not wait. But Peter didn't seem to mind his sermon being interrupted. The Holy Spirit is as gentle as a dove and respects our feelings in this matter.

Unbelief is often a hindrance. Jesus said, 'These signs will accompany *those who believe*... they will speak in new tongues' (Mk 16:17). As we shall be seeing, speaking in tongues requires faith whenever it is practised.

A final word, then, to Christians seeking this blessing. Do now allow any of these things to rob you of the wonderful sign of this blessing which will continue to be a help to you through the Christian life.

The gift is not meant *only* as a sign of blessing, though for many it fulfils that function well. It should be continuously used in prayer and praise, as a powerful tool in the service of the Lord. There are many times when, as Paul indicates in Romans 8:26, we neither know *how* to pray nor *what* to pray for, and so the Holy Spirit will help us in our weakness. There is always a need in our lives for Spirit-directed praying, and the gift of speaking in tongues is a great help. This is all the more reason why we should desire to have this gift, and why it is often given when we are filled with the Holy Spirit.

Conditions of receiving

So far we have seen how the early Christians received this blessing. It is available today as it was then. Peter made this clear at the outset—'the promise is to . . . every one whom the Lord our God calls to him' (Acts 2:39). If the blessing is the same, then we can take it that the conditions will be also.

The basic condition Jesus makes is *thirst*. There is no doubt that it is this which is leading so many of God's people to seek for the fullness of the Spirit today. Thirst aptly describes their spiritual condition. Their life is like a desert. They feel dry and desiccated. They may have lost their first love, their enthusiasm for Jesus Christ and his service. They have more of the spirit of slavery than that of sonship. Their prayer life is dull and monotonous. So they long for the rivers of living water that can turn their desert into fruitfulness. It is clear from the words of Jesus that intellectual interest or conviction is not enough; important though this is, it must be matched by that deep inner longing for reality and the power clearly promised to all Christians.

1. *Repentance*. 'Repent,' said Peter, '. . . and you shall receive the gift of the Holy Spirit' (Acts 2:38). Repentance is not the most popular word in the English language. It conjures up the most negative feelings in us, and we tend either to ignore it or to become so tense about it that it has the wrong kind of influence over us and keeps us in a permanent condition of despair and condemnation. But in actual fact it is a word we ought to welcome; for it has always been God's way back for his people and should be associated with joy rather than sadness. Only when we resist or resent what God is

60

calling us to does the whole experience become bad for us.

Many years ago a friend of mine visited the Mary Sisters of Darmstadt, where we had heard they laid great stress on repentance. I was interested to hear about his impressions. He assured me that the reports were true, but 'they are so joyful about it' he reassured me. When I visited Darmstadt for the first time I knew exactly what he meant. Here was a community of people who had discovered that the way of repentance was the way of joy.

A simple and sincere repentance is necessary to receive God's blessing. In the early church as we have seen the baptism in the Spirit was received normally at or very soon after conversion and water baptism—so the repentance necessary before there could be faith in Christ and baptism in water would have sufficed for this blessing too. But our situation may be different, since often time elapses between conversion and the baptism in the Spirit, sometimes many years, and unconfessed sin hinders the receiving of this blessing. Confession, renunciation of all known sin and if necessary restitution may have to precede this blessing, and we need to ask God to search our hearts, so that we know whether this is true or not.

In Acts 5:32 Peter and the apostles told the High Priest that God gave the Holy Spirit 'to those who obey him'. Obedience, therefore, is another condition of receiving 'the promise of the Father'. Any form of rebelliousness against God or what he has allowed us to experience in life, or against any part of his revealed word or laws, will hinder us from receiving this blessing.

2. *Belief.* The promised Holy Spirit is for all whom God calls to himself—in other words every committed Christian. Jesus made it clear that the Holy Spirit could not be received by everyone. In speaking of the Spirit of truth, he said that the world could not receive him 'because it neither sees him nor knows him' (Jn 14:17). Church membership is not enough; we must know Christ as our personal Saviour and Lord before we are eligible to receive this blessing. Paul was careful to tell the twelve disciples of Ephesus about Jesus Christ before he was able to lay his hands upon them to receive the Holy Spirit.

We see this clearly in Paul's letter to the Galatians. Paul writes, *'Because you are sons,* God has sent the Spirit of his Son into our hearts, crying, "Abba, Father"' (Gal 4:6). It is on the grounds of our sonship with God that we can pray that the Spirit of his Son should come into our hearts. Likewise in Luke 11:13 Jesus says that if our earthly fathers know how to give good things to their children, 'how much more will the heavenly Father give the Holy Spirit to those who ask him.'

We must first believe in Christ for our forgiveness and justification—and then the blessing can be ours. Indeed the purpose, among other things, of our being redeemed from 'the curse of the law' is that 'in Christ Jesus the blessing of Abraham might come upon the Gentiles, *that we might receive the promise of the Spirit through faith'* (Gal 3:13-14).

But we also need to see 'belief' as part of our commitment to the lordship of Jesus. There were not two kinds of Christians in the New Testament—the committed and the 'passengers', the active and the passive. To say

'Jesus is Lord' meant everything to Christians then and to become a Christian sometimes cost them their lives. The church thrives when people really believe and trust Jesus Christ as Lord, but that faith needs to be part of something wider and larger—a commitment to a life of obedience to Christ.

3. *Faith*. '... and be baptized every one of you in the name of Jesus Christ for the forgiveness of your sins; and you shall receive the gift of the Holy Spirit' (Acts 2:38).

Faith is necessary for both baptism and the receiving of the Spirit. 'He who believes and is baptized will be saved,' said Jesus—and he will not recognize baptism as valid without faith. The commandment of the Head of the church was that his people should 'make disciples' and then baptize them in the name of the Trinity (Mt 28:19). Alas, there are many baptized people today both inside and outside our churches who do not have a personal faith in Jesus Christ. But faith is also essential for the reception of this blessing of the Holy Spirit. The coming of the Holy Spirit on the day of Pentecost was in response to the disciples' faith in Jesus Christ. For Peter, when reporting to the church at Jerusalem what had happened in the home of Cornelius, said that God had given the same gift to them 'as he gave to us when we believed in the Lord Jesus Christ' (Acts 11:17).

Paul had to remind the Christians in Galatia, who were becoming infected with legalism, that they received the Holy Spirit 'by hearing with faith' (Gal 3:2,5). The ability to speak in tongues which often accompanies the receiving of this blessing is as we have seen, also given by the Holy Spirit in answer to our faith —'these signs will accompany those who believe...

63

they will speak in new tongues' (Mk 16:17).

We must, therefore, first see the promise as a word from Christ and then take a step of faith and receive what he has promised. 'We conclude,' says Paul, 'that faith is awakened by the message, and the message that awakens it comes through the word of Christ' (Romans 10:17 New English Bible). Let the word of Christ, 'I will send the Holy Spirit to you', ring in our ears and awaken faith in us to receive the promise (Jn 15:26).

4. *Prayer*. It is interesting and revealing to notice how often prayer is associated with this blessing. It is noticeable, for instance, that Jesus himself was in prayer when the Holy Spirit came upon him at his baptism in Jordan (Luke 3:21-22). Jesus tells us that the Father gives the Holy Spirit 'to those who ask him' (Luke 11:13). Now the context of this verse is important. Jesus had just told the parable of the friend who comes at night hungry and in search of hospitality, and this parable is clearly linked with the parable that follows it about a father and his children, and both are about prayer. But we need to notice that the friend is given food at midnight not because he is his friend but because of his 'importunity'. The primary meaning of this word apparently is 'shamelessness'. Dr R. A. Torrey comments, 'It is the persistent determination in prayer to God that will not be put to shame by any apparent refusal on God's part to grant the thing that we ask.'[15] We may need the spirit of wrestling Jacob, who would not let God go until he had blessed him (Gen 32:26). But let us beware of thinking that we shall be heard for our 'much praying', or the intensity of this praying. God always looks on the heart, and when he

sees that our heart's desire is for this blessing he will give it to us. But when our mind and not our heart is in it—we may well have to wait.

We will always find, when we look back on our search for this promise of God to his people, that the reasons why we don't receive immediately are always our own failures—never God's. So many of us have been brought up as Christians not to expect God to honour his word or keep his promises, so that we are very surprised when he does. It is as true today as it was in Jesus' day that faith is sometimes to be found more definitely among so-called 'unbelievers' than among those of us who claim to be 'believers'. God never fails his people. He is 100% reliable. But we fail God many times because of the weakness or shallowness of our faith.

Conclusion

There are no hard and fast techniques to this blessing. Naked faith based on the promise of Christ is the main ingredient. The laying-on of hands is certainly scriptural, but seems to have been optional in the early church and is definitely not a prerequisite. Some people receive on their own; others when they are prayed for, and the imposition of human hands does encourage faith and acts as a kind of 'human conductor' which many have found decisive when it comes to the moment of faith to receive this baptism in the Holy Spirit.

It is good to seek the help of others who have received this blessing. The record of the early church is clear that God does use others. It was Ananias who was commissioned by God to bring this blessing to Saul of

Tarsus, while Peter was told by the Holy Spirit to go to Caesarea to minister to Cornelius. Indeed the day of Pentecost is the only exception in the recorded instances where there is no human intermediary, though as this was the first occasion it is not surprising.

So we seek to fulfil the conditions and in prayer we ask the Father for the gift of the Holy Spirit and Jesus to baptize us in the same Spirit. As our prayer is answered and we are filled with the Holy Spirit, so we should begin to speak in tongues as the Spirit gives us utterance.

Finally, let us deal with the practical matter of how we actually speak in other tongues. There is much misunderstanding over this. Some people are puzzled as to whether it is we who speak or the Holy Spirit. The answer is—both. It is a glorious partnership. David du Plessis has put it simply: 'Without the Holy Spirit we cannot speak in tongues, without us the Holy Spirit will not.' Cecil Cousen has written about this:

> Speaking in tongues is a perfect illustration of the nature of the whole purpose of the enduement with power from on high... an ideal symbol of the communion of the Holy Spirit.... He has all the ability to speak in a language unknown to me.[16]

Let us then look closely at the one occasion in the New Testament when we are told *how* people spoke in tongues—the day of Pentecost. We are told 'they were all filled with the Holy Spirit and began to speak in other tongues, as the Spirit gave them utterance' (Acts 2:4). Here we see this delicate partnership at work. It is like a game of chess that two people play. One person makes the first move, *but cannot move again until his opponent has made his move.*

There are three moves in the baptism in the Holy Spirit. God *always* makes the first move, but will not make his second move (enabling us to speak in tongues) until we have made our move (and begin to speak). We must speak out in faith, however strange it may sound. Some people at Pentecost thought the disciples were drunk. We do not speak in English, for it is impossible to speak two languages at once. When we speak in tongues we do not use the mind to speak—Paul says that his mind was 'unfruitful' when he spoke in tongues (1 Cor 14:14)—but rather our mind concentrates on Jesus, and our lips are liberated by the Spirit to praise God in a new language.

When we begin to speak in tongues for the first time it is such a strange and unusual experience for us that we are tempted sometimes to carry out some immediate linguistic research. This means we stop speaking and have a good look at it. What is really happening is that we are taking our eyes off the Lord. Like Peter when he was walking on the water this usually proves fatal. Speaking in tongues is not given to us to titillate our intellects or to give us something new to *think about*. It is given as a tool to help us praise God and refresh our spirits. It opens up our spiritual life to new dimensions of usefulness and service of the Lord. It should, therefore, be used in the way it was intended. Once we have begun to speak we should not stop, but keep on going. Neither should we be satisfied with a few words or a slender vocabulary. The Lord wants us to have a full flowing prayer language, and so it is something that he will go on adding to in the coming days as we open up more and more of our life to him.

5

Living on the Promises

When we have been baptized in the Spirit it is important to realize that this is only the *start* of a new life—a life that means *living on the promises*. It is the beginning of a new and exciting life with boundless possibilities. It will open up for us many other promises. But equally it can all be ruined if we do not go on carefully and faithfully from the experience of the Spirit's fullness.

The Christian life at its most basic consists of believing in God's promises and obeying God's commands. Both belong together. To believe and not to obey will lead us to an unbalanced life, sometimes into the realm of fanaticism. We will be tempted to fantasize the Christian life and drift gradually into a grey area of unreality. However, simply to obey and not to believe will lead us into a rigid legalism, a dull and monotonous existence in which we will be increasingly bound by our unbelief. The Lord does not accept the one without the other, nor will he trade faith for obedience or obedience for faith.

As we have already seen, the reception of the baptism in the Holy Spirit is described in terms of both faith and obedience (compare Acts 11:17 and 5:32). The course that we now set will prosper and be fruitful to the extent we trust the Lord and obey him.

Another way of describing what happens to us after we have received this experience is 'enjoying the promise'. It is one thing to *receive* this great promise— and another thing to *enjoy* it.

Some may query the use of the word 'enjoy'. It has been used deliberately. The Westminster Shorter Catechism rightly asserts that the chief end of man is 'to glorify God and to enjoy him for ever'. The word may have been debased through modern usage, but there is nothing wrong with the basic idea of 'enjoying' our relationship with God. Receiving this promise lifts such enjoyment on to a new plane altogether. Worship which was tedious in public and almost non-existent in private becomes a blessed experience of joyful fellowship with the Father who loves us and the Son who abides in us. The Holy Spirit purifies our worship so that we can lose all consciousness of time and space and our wretched self-interests, and become 'lost in wonder, love and praise'.

The expression 'praise the Lord', which occupies such a prominent place in the Bible, finds its way often to our lips as we feel the love of God welling up from a full heart. We can become those rejoicing people who are the best advertisement possible for the Christian religion. But this enjoyment needs cultivating carefully. The great pastor of Kidderminster, Richard Baxter, in his book *The Saints' Everlasting Rest*, has a chapter entitled 'A directory for the getting and keeping of the heart in heaven'. This chapter, then, is concerned with keeping our hearts in heaven, where we have been made to sit with Christ, and avoiding pitfalls that may lie ahead of us.

There are some who argue that Christians should not seek this blessing since there is no commandment to do so in the epistles. But if you applied this argument logically you would do away with water baptism and the Lord's Supper as well, for neither of these is commanded in the epistles. There is a very simple reason for this. All Christians in those days were baptized in water and received the bread and wine in communion regularly. In Romans 6:3 Paul assumes that every true Christian has been baptized in water. Similarly in 1 Corinthians 11:17-18 Paul assumes that Christians attend Holy Communion. Nowhere does Paul command Christians to do so. And so for the same reason there are no commands in the epistles that Christians should seek a baptism in the Spirit—for in those days it was part of normal Christian initiation. The writers of the epistles would have assumed that everyone had received the power of the Spirit. They always refer back to this experience, reminding Christians of it rather than urging them to seek further experience in the future. For instance, writing to Timothy, Paul says, 'I remind you to rekindle the gift of God that is within you through the laying on of my hands' (2 Tim 1:6). And to the Corinthians he says that 'God has put his seal upon us and given us his Spirit in our hearts as a guarantee' (2 Cor 1:22). Again to the Ephesians, 'You... were sealed with the promised Holy Spirit' (Eph 1:13). But surely we are very much mistaken if we assume that this must be true for us because it was true for them. *Only if our experience is the same as theirs will such statements be true.*

Much has been written about the interpretation of 1 Corinthians 12:13, 'For by one Spirit we were all baptized into one body—Jews or Greeks, slaves or free—and all were made to drink of one Spirit.' Opinion is divided as to the meaning of this verse. There are some who believe that on its own it debunks the idea that Christians should seek a further baptism in the Spirit, since it says that it was an experience shared by everyone. But this verse is significantly different from the other references to being baptized in the Spirit. The order of the words is not the same and the context is different. Besides, the Greek preposition used here is notoriously difficult to translate, since it can mean a whole variety of things. Although it is the same word translated elsewhere 'in', it can equally well be translated 'by', as indeed the majority of modern translations have it. Anyway, even if it is a reference to what we have called elsewhere 'the baptism in the Holy Spirit' it still does not necessarily mean that all Christians today are baptized in the Spirit. Paul writes *'we were all'*, referring no doubt to himself and the Corinthians. *Only if our experience of the Holy Spirit is the same as theirs in depth and content would this be true today*. But, as we have already pointed out many times, Christians of today are often defective in many features, and sub-normal when compared with New Testament Christianity.

Let us give an example of this. If water baptism ceased to be practical in our churches, the fact that New Testament Christians practised it would make no difference to our practise of it, except to point to a glaring deficiency. So it is with Spirit baptism. Yes, it was the rule rather than the exception in the New

Testament that Christians were baptized in the Spirit. *It ought to be true today, but often isn't.* The New Testament record is there to challenge us to experience what New Testament Christians experienced, not to excuse ourselves from seeking what they had on the grounds that we all automatically receive it because we are Christians like them. This is why Paul does not urge his readers to be baptized in the Spirit. They were not so foolish as to think that they could do God's will without it.

Safeguards

Power is dangerous. It can destroy life as well as create it, divide Christians as well as unite them, offend unbelievers as well as draw them to Christ. We would be irresponsible if we thought that power can be given to immature people without serious risk to them and to others. But God is faithful to his word. He does honour his promises and gives power to all those who ask in faith. It is up to us to see that we honour and respect that trust and do not use the power he gives us wantonly or corruptly.

There are three main safeguards we need to accept for the healthy maintenance and development of this blessing in our lives. The first is to see that the Holy Spirit is given to us so that Jesus Christ is glorified, *not us*. Our own blessing is secondary, God's glory is primary. When self-interest or a party spirit begins to take over, the blessing evaporates.

Secondly, we need to see that Jesus promises this power to his people in order that they might be effective witnesses in the world. In a sense Pentecost was for the world, not for the church. The unconverted world witnessed the effect that Pentecost had on the church with remarkable results, as we shall see. The Holy Spirit is missionary-minded, and so should we be. To ignore the needs of the world around us is to grieve the Holy Spirit. If we do not co-operate with the Spirit's concern for the world, we shall lose his power.

The third safeguard is the Christian church. We cannot go it alone—we all need to be part of a fellowship of people who 'with one voice glorify the God and Father of our Lord Jesus Christ' (Rom 15:6). We shall receive most of our 'course corrections' through our involvement in the body of Christ as an active part of that body—a 'living stone' in the temple that God is building. God wants to use us not only as a witness in the world, but also as a contributor to the building up and maturing of the body of Christ. We shall be preserved from fanaticism and from following destructive false trails by our learning to submit humbly to our fellow believers in the body of Christ and the structure of leadership that exists in our church. There will probably be people who are older and wiser than ourselves, who have been blessed in the Spirit before us and know from experience that 'all that glitters is not gold'. We would be foolish to ignore their advice. We all need the kind of correction that submission to others inevitably brings with it.

We see the perfect demonstration of this, as we should expect, on the day of Pentecost itself. Here is a pattern for us to follow. We need to notice that the first reaction of the coming of the Holy Spirit upon the church was that they began speaking not to the world but to God in the unknown languages that the Holy

Spirit gave them, unselfishly losing themselves and worshipping in the Spirit. Such worship drew a crowd of well over three thousand. By modern standards it was disorderly and undignified—but where today does the worship of a church draw a crowd of three thousand un-believers? The joy of this experience was suddenly switched, with devastating effect, from God's direction to man's. Peter got up and preached in the power of the same Holy Spirit. This was not an experience to be selfishly enjoyed by a few, but to be shared with all. So the witness of the church began under the inspiration of the Holy Spirit. The miracle of tongues gave way to the miracle of three thousand converts. So it should always be.

But the miracles did not cease with the preaching of the gospel—there were more to come on that great day of Pentecost. Perhaps the greatest of the three was the creation of true fellowship in the body of Christ. Ponder these amazing words describing a church which had just been created: 'And all who believed were together and had all things in common' (Acts 2:44). There are many today speaking in tongues—there is much preaching of the gospel—but where do we find that kind of fellowship? We might call it mundane after the excitement of the tongues and the mass evangelism. But there would have been no continuation of Pente-costal blessing had not each Christian allowed his individuality to be merged into the whole body.

Jesus Christ came to save us from sin and death and give us eternal life. But he also came to mould us into a body, to build a church against which the gates of hell would not prevail. And the Holy Spirit comes not only to dwell in the temples of our bodies, but to form and motivate powerful groups of Christians who will be able to smash the kingdom of Satan.

It is essential that we grasp the full significance of this blessing if we are to enjoy it to the full. It is given that we might glorify God throughout our lives, that we might function properly and unselfishly in the body of Christ into which we have been baptized, and that we might be effective witnesses. These three safeguards should preserve us from the pitfalls and false paths which lie ahead of us.

Glorifying God

This experience of the Holy Spirit is in one sense an entering into the glory of God. I have seen people who have just been baptized in the Spirit whose faces have shone with the literal shekinah glory. When Moses was in the presence of God his face reflected his glory, and Paul tells us that the dispensation of the Holy Spirit should be attended with greater splendour even than that which Moses experienced (2 Corinthians 3:7-18).

After Jesus had been anointed with the power of the Holy Spirit he was immediately led by the same Spirit into the desert to be tempted by Satan. It seems that many Christians go the way of the Master after their baptism of power. Fierce doubts then assail them. Just as Satan's first words to Christ were, 'If you are the Son of God...', so he sows doubts in our minds. Nearly everyone is tempted to doubt their experience—especially the speaking in tongues. We must defeat such temptation, as Jesus did, with the word of God. This further underlines the importance of seeking what God promises rather than personal experiences. There is no reason why we should not come triumphantly through all trials with God's help.

It is important to continue to speak in tongues even if the vocabulary of the new language is limited. The Holy Spirit will extend this language as we go on *in faith*. We shall find, as Paul says, that we are edified according to our faith as we speak to God in this way. There are many different aspects of prayer for which this gift will prove invaluable. Of course we continue to pray with the mind, but alongside it we now have the complementary ability of praying with the spirit.

Most aspects of prayer are enhanced by the use of this gift. We shall be able to *worship* God more freely, because the gift of tongues enables us to take our mind off what we are saying and concentrate it more fully on the One to whom we are speaking. When it comes to *intercession*, this new gift helps us to pray more definitely—for we often do not know what to pray for or how to pray for people and situations. 'We do not know how to pray as we ought, but the Spirit himself intercedes for us with sighs too deep for words' (Rom 8:26). This may well be an actual reference to speaking in tongues, but in any case it points to our human frailty when interceding and assures us of the Holy Spirit's help. When we turn to *confession,* we are not always aware of exactly what we have been doing wrong. We are easily self-deceived. Here too the gift of tongues can help bring to our remembrance the things that need to be confessed. To cap it all the gift is a marvellous aid to *thanksgiving,* releasing us in new ways to appreciate all God's love and gifts to us. And Jesus, as we have seen, also mentioned it as a sign to unbelievers (Mk 16:17). Surely such a remarkably helpful gift should be coveted by all God's people.

But we need to beware of 'spiritual pride' (not that pride is ever spiritual). Speaking in tongues is not a sign of Christian maturity. As we have seen, it should normally accompany the beginning of Christian experience, so it is nothing to boast about. We shall find some Christians who do not speak in tongues who are more mature than ourselves, so let us not think of ourselves more highly than we ought to think, but 'think with sober judgment, each according to the measure of faith which God has assigned him' (Rom 12:3).

It is best to let your minister know as soon as possible. It is better for him to hear about it from you than from someone else, who might give him a wrong impression altogether. Our ministers are called by God to keep watch over our souls and they will have to give account to God for us (Heb 13:17), so it is only fair that we should share a deep blessing with them. If we are ministers it may be right to inform our superiors, colleagues and congregations. But we must be very careful when to do it. Bragging is a temptation—and also a principal source of leakage in power. Paul said to the Corinthians, 'The kingdom of God does not consist in talk but in power' (1 Cor 4:20). This experience is not given us to talk about—except with those who are interested and hungry—but to empower us for God's service.

Christians are commanded to be filled with the Spirit and to walk in the Spirit. This experience will be very shortlived and crowned with many disappointments if we do not maintain the glow. This means above all obediently waiting upon God. We must spend more time in his presence. If we obey the Spirit's prompting the length of our devotions will be extended, and we should allow for longer periods of waiting upon God.

Above all we should always carry with us 'the shield of faith' (Eph 6:16). The tragedy of the Galatian Christians was that although they had received the Spirit by faith, they soon lapsed into legalism. It is faith alone which enables us to keep in the full stream of the Holy Spirit's blessing, and each day will bring opportunities for exercising this faith.

Witnessing to the world

The church's first response to the coming of the Holy Spirit was to praise and glorify God in the languages which the Holy Spirit gave them. But if that had been all, the Church would not have lasted a decade. It would have gone down in history as just another Jewish sect. Sometimes people refer to 'the Tongues Movement' in these days. They mean either the Pentecostals or the present re-appearance of the gift of tongues in the historic denominations. If there is a movement (and I do not know of one) which is just concerned with speaking in tongues, then no one need treat it very seriously. Just as the tongues of praise on the day of Pentecost preceded the preaching of the gospel and the start of a miraculous ministry in the church, so it should be today.

It is vital to see that the promise of power is linked with witness—and if we do not witness, then we shall soon lose the power. Jesus said, 'You shall receive power when the Holy Spirit has come upon you, and you shall be my witnesses' (Acts 1:8). In Ephesus the twelve disciples did not meet solely to enjoy their new experience of speaking in tongues—they went out under the leadership of Paul so that in only two years 'all the residents of Asia heard the word of the Lord, both Jews and Greeks' (Acts 19:10). This is the purpose for which God gives us power, that out of our innermost beings might flow the rivers of living water. Bishop Westcott says in his commentary:

> The reception of the blessing leads at once to the distribution of it in fuller measure...he who drinks of the Spiritual Rock becomes in turn himself a rock from within which the waters flow to slake the thirst of others.[17]

The driving force behind the early outreach of the church was the Holy Spirit. It was he who broke down the barrier between Jews and Gentiles and led Peter to baptize the first non-Jews. It was the Holy Spirit who led Paul to preach in Europe. If we do not have a deep missionary compulsion, then we do not have the full blessing of the Holy Spirit—for he always gives this to us. And if we do not respond to this compulsion with eager concern for the unconverted, the power of the Spirit will soon depart from us.

Edifying the church

There were three miracles of the Holy Spirit on the day of Pentecost. We have already referred to the first two—the speaking in tongues and the conversion of the multitudes—and now we must consider the third. We are told, 'All who believed were together and had all things in common' (Acts 2:44). The Holy Spirit instantaneously created amazing fellowship. And this is the third great purpose of power—to cause the body of Christ to function properly.

It is most important for us to see this purpose for the baptism in the Holy Spirit alongside that of evangelism. For if we don't keep the Christian family in good shape the new members of the family drawn to Jesus Christ through evangelism will not be nourished or cared for. It is also vital that evangelists (who are usually quite few) and witnesses (who should include the entire church) are built up, encouraged and constantly being renewed in vision and spiritual strength, if evangelism is going to continue to be fruitful. Many Christians see the need for power in worship and witness, but how many have caught the vision of the body of Christ as a Spirit-filled community functioning spontaneously by the inspiration of the Spirit with spiritual ministries dovetailing into one another? For lack of this vision this blessing of the Holy Spirit can become very lopsided. Just as the Spirit will not bless for long the person who loses his concern for the unconverted, so the Holy Spirit will not operate as powerfully or completely in the lives of individuals as he will in the Christian community.

So to enjoy the blessing to the full we must be a member of a fellowship, contributing as the Spirit leads to the mutual upbuilding of the other members. It is the normal experience of those who have been filled with the Holy Spirit that when they meet together, among other things the Spirit gives manifestations for the good of all. These gifts of the Spirit are described in 1 Corinthians 12, Romans 12:6-8 and 1 Peter 4:10-11. They seem to be regarded in the New Testament as part of normal church life. Alas, our present day normality is so abnormal by New Testament standards that when the 'normal' takes place it is regarded with horror by some regular churchgoers. Instead of being greeted with joy and thankfulness the gifts of the Spirit have been known to cause the utmost alarm. But this ignorance and fear is being gradually overcome.

In these first chapters we are dealing with the blessing called the baptism in the Holy Spirit. In the next chapter we shall deal practically with the question of spiritual gifts.

Which church should I belong to?

In the last few years some people have left the churches they belonged to when they were blessed, and have transferred their allegiance to another church nearby, or have even moved out of the district altogether in order to join a sympathetic church. Others have remained members of their churches in spite of the fact that they have had little understanding or help in the new and exciting experience which they have received. Not a few have been the means of bringing others into blessing, and in some cases they have gradually seen their whole church blessed and renewed in the Spirit. Of course this is the ideal, but all too often it does not happen. Some years back there was a polarization between so-called 'stay-inners' and 'come-outers', but that is no longer the case, and most people have come to realize that to be dogmatic either way is wrong. Clearly some have been called to stay in, others to come out. But all need to be sure they are hearing the Lord accurately, for he is the Head of the church, and if we hear 'marching orders', then we should be careful to find out whether it is really God speaking or whether we are just pursuing the line of least resistance, or just chickening out of a difficult situation.

The charismatic renewal has been going long enough for two facts to be established. First, that the decision that many have made to stay in has paid off, so that the renewal has become firmly planted in some local churches. Secondly, that the decision that others have made to leave has also paid off, so that they have become well established in other churches where they have been able to grow and become strong in the Lord. Some of these churches are new and independent ones, others are members of the denominations. So no hard and fast rule can be made which would bind everyone. Each person needs to find out the will of God for himself.

There are some who experience the power of the Holy Spirit after many years as Christians. They have a maturity which is able to sustain them through what often can be a wilderness experience. Others are young in the faith and not well equipped to go through the hardships of persecution and misunderstanding which sometimes takes place when we remain within an unrenewed local church. For them the right thing might be to leave and join a charismatic church, if there is one near at hand, or at least a church where there is sound teaching and a committed fellowship of believers.

But quite often there is a middle course we can take—to belong to an unrenewed church and at the same time to attend regularly either an ecumenical charismatic prayer group or the local days of renewal that are often these days arranged for teaching and fellowship. Thus we can stay to be a blessing in our own church, while at the same time get regular encouragement and strengthening in various renewal meetings and conferences. The end that God has in mind is not Spirit-filled individuals but Spirit-filled communities. The power from the prayers of such groups will again turn the world upside down.

6

When You Come Together

One of the first problems which seems to face Christians after they have been filled with the Holy Spirit, is how to go on into the experience of the gifts of the Spirit.

It seems that there are three ingredients which need to be present if a church or fellowship is to reap the full benefit of the whole gamut of spiritual gifts. The first is *love*. Each member of the fellowship should be lovingly concerned for the welfare of the other members. 'Love one another with brotherly affection,' Paul exhorts the Christians in Rome—'outdo one another in showing honour' (12:10). 'Do nothing from selfishness or conceit, but in humility count others better than yourselves. Let each of you look not only to his own interests, but also to the interests of others,' he tells the Philippians (2:3-4). If these gifts are 'for the common good', then a deep concern for others will be the best incentive for the gifts to be manifested. If we come to meetings only concerned for our own blessing, then we shall not be the right channels for the Holy Spirit to use to edify others. It is humility of mind, which Paul calls the mind of Christ in his letter to the Philippians, which is the essential basis of truly effective fellowship.

The second ingredient should be *faith*. As we have already seen, these gifts are not human talents, but activities directly related to the Holy Spirit. Now the Holy Spirit never sets aside or overrides the human personality, as is the experience of spiritist mediums. When we manifest one of the vocal gifts, we do all the speaking, but the Spirit gives us the words to speak. On our side, faith is the essential quality required if these gifts are to be manifested. Paul tells the Romans (12:6), 'if prophecy, *in proportion to our faith*'. If there is little faith, there will be little or no prophecy. We shall deal later with the matter of how we know when we have an 'anointing' to manifest a gift. But when we are prompted by the Spirit to do so, our faith has to respond if the gift is to operate. As we speak, so more words will be given to us. A strong faith in God is essential if the gifts are to flourish in our churches. A timid and shy attitude will tend to quench the Spirit.

The third ingredient is *time*. We must allow time for the Holy Spirit to work in our midst. It is in this area that we often fail. The hastily conducted prayer meeting, the closely scheduled service of worship, the Christian with one eye on the clock all the time, will not experience the full blessings which God has for those of his children who take the trouble to wait long enough on him. And, if such gatherings are closely packed with prayers, and there are no periods of silence, then the Holy Spirit will very probably not be able to speak through us. The still small voice will not be heard, and

85

the message will not get through. Longer time together will never be wasted, for lack of concentrated prayer is a major source of weakness in our churches. I have also known occasions when a real spiritual breakthrough has been imminent, and the whole atmosphere has changed like a punctured balloon when a spiritually insensitive leader has interrupted, or an undiscerning Christian has prayed in an irrelevant or carnal fashion. The moments of greatest power in a meeting will very often be in those times of silence when we are most open to the Spirit's inspiration.

There are some definite hindrances too which need to be dealt with. Initially, for instance, it is easy to fall into this trap: because of the comparative novelty of such gifts and ministry, there may be a tendency to become so preoccupied with them that the whole purpose of meeting together is forgotten. The purpose should be to meet with God in worship and prayer, *not* to enjoy spiritual gifts for their own sake. In other words there can be a fatal concentration of attention on gifts instead of on the Giver. The results of this confusion may well be disastrous. Such meetings degenerate into little more than psychic fellowships. But no group need feel 'cheated' if no spiritual gifts are manifested. These are the responsibility of the Holy Spirit and in his sovereign discretion he may choose to withhold such gifts temporarily, especially if they are becoming the centre of attraction. The Spirit desires to glorify the Son, and is jealous that he should have the pre-eminence in every meeting of God's people. The gifts should never become an end in themselves, or they will soon disappear.

Bad relationships will also be a hindrance to the

operation of spiritual gifts. There must be a high regard for the corporate good. If we come to meetings or services with resentment in our hearts for others, or a spirit of criticism, or bad feeling against others, at best it will mar the blessing and power of the gathering, but at worst this unloving spirit can be mixed with the gifts, and the Spirit will be grieved. Damage may well be done to others. As Jesus said, 'If you are offering your gift at the altar, and there remember that your brother has something against you, leave your gift there before the altar and go; first be reconciled to your brother, and then come and offer your gift' (Mt 5:23-24). If we have malice, spite or an uncharitable spirit, it will spoil what the Holy Spirit desires to do in such a gathering.

Decently and in order

Now a few practical points about the manner in which these gifts should be manifested. The principles have been clearly laid down by Paul: 'Let all things be done for edification' and 'all things should be done decently and in order' (1 Cor 14:26, 40). We have already covered the first of these, but the second is equally important.

Just as we hand presents graciously to those we love, wrapping them up at Christmas in bright coloured paper, and do not thrust them rudely at them, so we should manifest spiritual gifts 'decently'. This means we shall not shout unnaturally words of prophecy, nor speak so quietly that no one can properly hear us. It means we will not lay hands violently on people for healing, but gently and reverently. It needs to be said here that the laying-on of hands should be carefully ordered in the churches. The minister and other leaders in each church should specify who should have this ministry. These checks are necessary because it is so obviously open to abuse. 'Love is not arrogant or rude.' We shall avoid the crudities of some, who shake people and in other ways manipulate them, and seem to show themselves impervious to the sensitivities of those to whom they are ministering.

We should also observe the principle of orderliness. 'God is not a God of confusion but of peace,' Paul reminds the Corinthians (1 Cor 14:33). We may receive, for example, an anointing to manifest a gift during a service, but that does not mean that we have to do so there and then. We can wait until an appropriate opportunity presents itself. In our walk in the Spirit we must try to be sensitive to the views and feelings of others, especially those whom Paul calls 'unlearned'—which probably means those who do not understand or appreciate the gifts of the Spirit. The law of love should operate at all times.

Anointings

Some are perplexed as to when they should manifest one of the vocal gifts of the Spirit. How does one know, for instance, when the gift of tongues, which in its private use may be exercised as freely as prayer in English, should be manifested in public? Normally we do this when we have an 'anointing' as many people call it. It may come to us in various ways, but generally speaking it is a kind of pressure to do it, which does not come from ourselves. It is never compulsive, a power forcing us to do something, for Paul says that 'the spirits of prophets are subject to prophets' (1 Cor 14:32). This factor is one which distinguishes Christian gifts from the spiritist and occult, where there is a compelling spirit.

There is often a feeling of discomfort until the gift is manifested. It is impossible to describe what is bound to be very subjective, but it will be made clear to us at the time, and we learn gradually from experience when this is. If it is prophecy or interpretation, then usually the first words are given to us; they come into our minds without premeditation, but with real persistence. We have to venture forth in faith, speaking out the words that are given before more words come to us. It is rather like the packets of cleaning tissues you buy in the shops: when one tissue is removed from the box, another one follows it, and so the process is repeated. We shall learn to be sensitive to the Holy Spirit and his lead to us to begin speaking. But we must not forget to *stop* speaking also at the right time. Some people, warming to their message, continue after the anointing has passed, and the message ceases to be edifying.

Things to avoid

One of the things to be avoided, which can constitute a hindrance, is the unnecessary perpetuating of traditional ways of operating the gifts of the Spirit. For example, sometimes people will preface or conclude a prophecy with the words 'Thus saith the Lord'. This is perfectly innocent and is intended as a kind of 'signature tune' to prepare the listeners for what is to follow. But is it really necessary? It may be interpreted by some as being presumptuous to use the words of the

Old Testament prophets. It may also lead people to accept a prophecy as possessing inerrancy. It is much harder to 'weigh' what has been said, as Paul urges all listeners to do, when the person prophesying categorically states that it is the Lord speaking. It is perhaps better to leave these words out. But we should not deduce from this that God's voice has any less authority when he speaks through prophecy. A prophecy given at a meeting does not have universal and eternal application as Scripture has. But the main difference is that when there is a prophecy I must judge whether it really is God speaking or not. When I read the Scriptures I know that it is God's word.

In some churches it is customary to punctuate prayers or sermons with loud 'amens' and 'hallelujahs', etc. This can be very distracting to the one who is leading in prayer or exhortation, as well as to the congregation, each member of which should be following what the one who is leading is saying. It has become a well-established tradition with some, but it is another of those traditions which should not be imitated. It makes it very difficult for those unaccustomed to it to concentrate, and can quench the Spirit, since it all too often becomes an automatic reflex action and as ritualistic as mumbling prayers is to others. Words which are said without meaning them show an insensitiveness to the Holy Spirit.

Another tradition to use sparingly is the practice of speaking in tongues during a meeting, without interpretation and in concert. It may be edifying to the individual, but it certainly is not to the church, which is the reason why it is forbidden, since it breaks the scriptural principle for congregational worship: 'Let *all* things be done for edification' (1 Cor 14:26). Adherence to this rule is most important, otherwise meetings can develop into pandemonium, which grieves the Holy Spirit and offends many who are present, especially strangers. In moments of silence or at times when individual expressions of corporate worship are being used, it is still possible to pray in tongues without making a sound to distract others. Hannah is a good example here. We are told that as she continued 'praying before the Lord', Eli the priest 'observed her mouth. Hannah was speaking in her heart; only her lips moved, *and her voice was not heard*; therefore Eli took her to be a drunken woman' (1 Sam 1:12-13).

There does, however, seem to be one exception to this general rule. 'Singing with the spirit', as Paul calls it in 1 Cor 14:15, is similar to speaking in tongues, only the Holy Spirit in this case inspires not only the words but the music. As such it can be exercised in private (like a solo!) or in public, when many may be led to join in. The Holy Spirit becomes the choirmaster of a heavenly choir, and if the choirmaster is followed obediently, the resulting harmony of sound will be most edifying to those present, whether they are members of this choir or not.

Reverting to unhelpful traditions, John Wesley had to deal with similar problems which, while fairly harmless in themselves, could be distracting to others. For instance, he refers in his Journals to the practice of 'leaping up and down' which some of his more zealous members at times indulged in:

They are honest and upright men, who really feel the love of God in their hearts. But they have little experience either of the ways of God or the devices of Satan. So he serves himself of their simplicity, in order to wear them out and to bring a discredit on the work of God.

Maybe our approach should be as charitable and wise as that of John Wesley.

But we should all seek to be 'naturally supernatural' as someone has put it. These gifts and manifestations should not be unusual, but part of the normal ministry of the church. We should neither elevate them to a place of unscriptural prominence, nor grieve the Holy Spirit, who gives them to us, by denying their value or forbidding their operation. Let us neither fear nor despise them; and if God should choose to grant 'extraordinary miracles' as he did at Ephesus, then let us praise him for these too. But we shall not go far wrong if we obey the Pauline command to make love our aim and earnestly desire the spiritual gifts, while at the same time applying his principles that everything should be done decently and in order and for the edification of the church.

7

Members One of Another

As Jesus moved around Palestine proclaiming in word and deed the gospel of the kingdom, he was obviously limited by his physical body. He could not be in two places at the same time. When he was healing the sick in Capernaum, he could not be preaching in Nazareth. His healing ministry was restricted, apart from the short missions of the Twelve and Seventy, to his own two hands and compassionate heart.

And it is the same today. Jesus is still more or less restricted by his body. The only difference now is that his body can be in Capernaum and Nazareth at the same time, and indeed London and New York, or any other place you care to name. For the church is the body of Christ. It is important to notice that Paul does not say that the local church is *like* Jesus' body, but that *it is* (1 Cor 12:27). We are his hands and feet, and humanly speaking, he continues his normal ministry through his body—that is, the church, either in its universal or local expressions.

93

There has been considerable theological debate about the meaning of the word 'body' in Paul's writings. But the fact remains that Christ and his people are inextricably bound together, and he continues his great work through his people whether we are his body, in the sense I have described it, or he is the body. For an outline of the various arguments of the scholars see *The Body of Christ* by Alan Cole. [18]

This emphasizes the need for both local church unity and the functioning of the *whole* body. Jesus' body on earth was a perfect unity, with every part functioning properly, otherwise he would never have been able to do his work successfully. Only a local church functioning harmoniously is able to reveal to the world the full splendour of Christ. He cannot be seen fully in the life of a single individual. A group will always be a better witness than an individual.

Today, when so much is made of our 'painful divisions', and when the emphasis is on the denominational aspect of this, we need to see the harm that is also caused by division in a local church or Christian fellowship. It may be harder to establish a true unity here than in the wider field of ecumenism. But it is in the local church situation that the more direct concentration of witness is being made, and it is this unity which is the special target of Satan's divisive tactics. When Paul was facing this kind of threat, he wrote, 'We are not ignorant of his designs.'

Now this does have a practical bearing on our subject. For the almost automatic rejoinder by many when they hear of people receiving blessings and gifts of the Holy Spirit is, 'It's divisive.' Now, we must be honest. This certainly can be and has been divisive. On occasions it has severely hampered the work of God by splitting churches and fellowships into warring cliques. It is because of this that many regard the whole subject as distracting and unnecessary. We have to persuade people otherwise, for where there is love *on both sides* this is not divisive. For the essence of the Holy Spirit's work is to unite rather than divide the body of Christ. The trouble in Corinth was caused by some who were making too much of the gift of tongues, and perhaps others who wanted to forbid this gift altogether. To the first Paul says: 'Seek the other gifts, especially those that edify others,' and to the others, 'Do not forbid speaking in tongues.'

It is important to concentrate on the facts that unite Christians, rather than allow secondary considerations to divide. The basis of our unity is a common participation in Christ—the realization that in him we are 'members one of another' *not* because we all have the same kind of spiritual experience. It may follow that those who have been filled with the Spirit experience a deeper level of fellowship. But the baptism in the Spirit should never be allowed to be the grounds for dividing Christians from one another. Any examination of revivals reveals the divisive tendencies which are endemic with such experiences. It is not long before the phrase 'He is one of us' implies that cliquishness which we should do all we can to avoid.

Max Warren writes of an important attitude of mind which we should cultivate towards the subject of revival: we should deliberately refuse

to associate some inevitable connection between revival and schism. Experience suggests that we get what we genuinely expect. An attitude of humble expectancy towards the Holy Spirit in revival will bring a reformed and revived church. [19]

Above all we must carefully distinguish between the wheat and the chaff and not lump all together, which is, of course, a much easier way of dealing with the situation. Max Warren, in another section of his book, refuses to accept the inevitability of schism in revival. His words are worth weighing carefully, especially by those who are critical of any signs of 'enthusiasm'. He writes:

> The Church has the difficult duty of accepting the challenge of reformation, while at the same time distinguishing between the challenge which must be accepted and the idiosyncrasies of 'enthusiasm' which should be tested and may be rejected.

The exercise of the gifts of the Spirit is sometimes raised for division. There are some who argue, 'If you cannot exercise these gifts, you should leave your church or fellowship and join one where they are accepted.' Some may even go further and say that if you do not do this you will be guilty of quenching the Spirit. Such an attitude is misguided, although it appears at first sight to be reasonable or even inevitable. Is it not based on false assumptions? The first is that spiritual gifts are essential to the church. Now it is certainly true that they are essential for the proper functioning of the body of Christ. Theologians sometimes distinguish between what is essential to the church (the *esse*), and what is non-essential (the *bene esse*). Using this distinction we would say that the gifts of the Spirit are not essential to the existence of the church, only to its well-being.

The second false assumption is that *we* are quenching the Spirit if we do not manifest the gifts, even though it is in an unsympathetic fellowship. Under these circumstances surely it is *they* who are quenching the Spirit, not ourselves. For the gifts are for them, not for the ones who are manifesting them. If people are unprepared to accept these gifts, then we shall be guilty of quenching the Spirit of love if we force them on them before they are ready. Rather we should patiently pray that they will speedily come to see the value of them, and be prepared to accept them gratefully as gifts of God. In 1 Corinthians 13 Paul tells us that love 'does not insist on its own way'. To do so under these circumstances will hinder rather than help the work of the Spirit. Paul also defines love as being 'patient and kind'. If we shake the dust off our feet at our brethren, and move off somewhere else, what kind of love is that? The Holy Spirit is grieved by such impatience. At times we may well have to weep over the people of God, who refuse the blessings that God would give them, just as Jesus wept when he looked down on Jerusalem.

Nevertheless, the operation of the gifts of the Spirit within the normal fellowship of the church should be our regular experience, and every church which is concerned to conform to the pattern of the New Testament should expect to see them manifested in an atmosphere of love, and be disappointed if they are not in evidence.

The question is often asked as to whether or not these gifts should be manifested in the normal church services on Sundays, or reserved for the smaller mid-week gatherings. A quick look at the New Testament should leave us in no doubt that they were as much a part of regular worship as the Lord's Supper, and no distinction is ever made between Sunday and week-night meetings. Whenever the church meets for fellowship the Holy Spirit may desire to manifest some of the gifts. But our situation is very different from those early days. For one thing, they normally met in houses, not in large buildings where it is so much harder to create the kind of atmosphere where the gifts can operate freely. Vocal gifts will not edify the congregation if they are inaudible to most of those present. The ideal envisaged in 1 Corinthians 14 is full congregational worship, with every member contributing to the edification of the whole body. But owing to spiritual decline in the church, and the rise of ministerial domination, the proper functioning of the local church, when it gathers together, has been hopelessly stifled. The Church of England is by no means the only culprit here. Free Churches are equally hamstrung by the priestly notion of the one-man ministry.

But this situation can be changed, and there are signs in a number of directions that this is taking place. Those used to a free type of service can easily allow more participation by the congregation in the services of worship, and the gifts of the Spirit can be manifested in such a situation; while in the Church of England it has already been demonstrated that there is no need to dispense with the liturgy to make room for them. In future services we ought to allow more scope for an enlightened congregation to take part, as is indeed already being done in many churches. Extempore prayer should be allowed, and a time can easily be set apart for the exercise of spiritual gifts in either the communion service or the morning and evening services, provided, of course, the congregation understands what is going on, and is prepared to accept them as gifts of God.

In this connection it is important to remember that the person who has the gift does not have to manifest it compulsively, maybe at an inappropriate moment in the service. We have seen that 'the spirits of prophets are subject to prophets'. The person can wait until a suitable time is reached, and then manifest the gift. The gifts are for the whole local community, and are not primarily intended for a small and exclusive charismatic club outside the main fellowship. Anglicans are fortunate in possessing scriptural services, which form a splendid framework within which the gifts of the Spirit can operate to the glory of God without detracting from the liturgy itself.

We should notice that Paul does not encourage an uncritical attitude to these manifestations. Gullibility is not a Christian virtue. The church is to judge the utterances of all its members by the touchstone of Scripture, and this includes spiritual gifts as well as sermons. Paul says 'test everything' (1 Thess 5:21). In an atmosphere of love, there should be no friction in such 'judging'. And the meeting together of God's people should be preserved from exploitation by those who like Diotrephes love 'to have the pre-eminence' (3 John 9 AV). There are always some who love to hear the sound of their own voices. A wise minister will lovingly restrain and counsel such people, and encourage the humbler and perhaps more diffident brethren to manifest their gifts for the building up of the body.

It is an almost universal feature of the present wave of new blessing coming to God's people that there is an intense longing for deeper fellowship than is sometimes possible in our churches. It was true in East Africa in the revival—where the 'saved' Christians, who became known as the *balokali*, met for special fellowship, where they could confess, testify, sing, and praise their Lord. There is surely no harm in such meetings, as long as the dangers of divisiveness are remembered. If such a group develops in a local church, it should do so with the knowledge and permission of the minister and elders. There are few things more dangerous in a church than a secret society, which will be discovered sooner or later after rumours and misrepresentation have done their worst. Sometimes people may meet together who are members of different local churches. Again, there is nothing wrong, and indeed much blessing can flow from these meetings. But the dangers should not be forgotten. This kind of group can become a substitute for a local church, and would, therefore, sap rather than strengthen the churches. They can easily develop into 'holy huddles', concerned only with a narrow aspect of truth, instead of fellowships where Christians can rekindle the gift of the Spirit within them, and go back to their local church with greater strength than they had before.

It must always be remembered that the power of the Holy Spirit is given primarily that we might be witnesses to Christ. Even the building up of the fellowship should have this intention, rather than the cultivation of individual piety. And both evangelism and fellowship—as indeed everything we do—should have the same great purpose, the glorification of the Son of God.

8

Weak though Anointed

It was King David who, after the murder of Abner, said in his grief, 'I am this day weak, though anointed king' (2 Sam 3:39). One of the great qualities of David was his constant recognition of his own weakness. Although God had conferred great power and authority upon him, he knew that in himself there was no strength.

The most dangerous condition we can ever get ourselves into is to imagine that we are strong. 'Pride goes before destruction, and a haughty spirit before a fall,' says the writer of the Proverbs (16:18). The baptism in the Spirit is not a mark of Christian superiority, but if anything it underlines our weakness. It is because we are weak that we have had to seek for God's anointing. And when we have been blessed we do not ourselves get an ounce stronger. It is only that God's strength is able to flow more freely through us. But the danger of human pride will lurk all the time in the shadow of our forward progress. Pride is a deadly sin, and great has been the fall of some who have become its victim after experiencing great spiritual blessing.

One of the clearest examples of this comes in the Old Testament. We are told about King Uzziah that 'as long as he sought the Lord, God made him prosper' (2 Chron 26:5). We learn that 'his fame spread far, for he was marvellously helped, *till he was strong*' (2 Chron 26:15). There was nothing wrong with that strength, for it had been given him by God. But there came a day when, we read, 'he grew proud'. He began to attribute his strength to himself, and it led to his ultimate destruction, exactly as the verse we have quoted from Proverbs shows.

But it is important to notice the form his pride took. He went into the temple to burn incense, which the sons of Aaron alone were permitted to do. They had been consecrated for that work. But Uzziah presumed that he could even approach God with impunity. He went beyond the bounds and forgot his human weakness and sin. His fall came when he thought he was too important and too spiritual. Even then, he might have escaped judgement. Azariah the priest and no less than eighty of his assistants followed the King into the temple and rebuked him. But the King was too proud to listen to advice and to admit inadequacy before such a company of 'experts'. He lost his temper, and immediately became a leper. His punishment was exclusion from the house of the Lord for the rest of his life.

This story has been re-enacted time and time again. It is being repeated in the lives of Christians today. God makes men and women strong in the power of the Holy Spirit. They prosper. And instead of constantly acknowledging their natural weakness and humbling themselves before God, they become first proud and then arrogant, and finally presumptuous in the presence of God. They become intoxicated with the wine of success and popularity. They think they are virtually inerrant and indestructible. Like Uzziah, they are angry when others, seeing pride in them, admonish them. They think themselves above correction. Then comes the sickening fall. They have gone too far, and they suffer the horrors of spiritual leprosy and so exclusion from God's blessing and service. As Paul warned the Corinthians, having preached to others they have become 'disqualified' in the race of life (1 Cor 9:27).

Paul was an outstanding example of one who knew his own weaknesses, and counted only on God's strength. It was in the school of suffering that he learnt this supreme lesson, so that he thanked God for his thorn in the flesh, whatever that may have been. He did not come swaggering into Corinth on the crest of an advertising wave. 'I was with you in weakness and in much fear and trembling,' he reminded the Corinthians (1 Cor 2:3). But the results which flowed from his one-man mission put our evangelistic campaigns and missions to shame. Yet the converts he won in that city were later tempted to despise Paul because he had a weak physique, was unimpressive in appearance and his speech was 'of no account'.

Paul never gave up because of human weakness, nor did he become proud and presumptuous when God poured his power into his earthen vessel, as Paul himself called it, 'to show that the transcendent power belongs to God and not to us' (2 Cor 4:7). He rejoiced in his weakness, for when he was weak, then he was strong (2 Cor 12:10). He would boast of his weaknesses rather than his strength, knowing that only then would the power of Christ rest upon him.

Hudson Taylor, the founder of one of the world's largest missionary societies and the first Protestant to evangelize inland China, knew this experience too, and never forgot it to his dying day. 'All God's giants,' he once wrote, 'have been weak men who did great things for God because they reckoned on his being with them. They counted on God's faithfulness.'

When we are baptized in the Spirit, we are just beginning. We are going to make many mistakes. We shall have our failures as well as successes and triumphs. We must never allow these successes to make us proud. We must give God *all* the glory, and not talk too much about them. Nevertheless, we must never allow our failures to lead us to despair or resignation. They too should be stepping-stones along the way of faith, rather than stumbling-blocks. If we are humble we shall learn from these mistakes. The proud man seldom acknowledges failure, and so never learns from it, for he thinks he knows all the answers. He will seldom take advice, and becomes angry when corrected. If we are going to be of any use to God, we must possess the humility to learn from others.

Though we have been anointed with the mighty Holy Spirit, we are still weak and 'nothing good dwells within me, that is, in my flesh' (Rom 7:18). Every moment we need the presence and power of God. Jesus said 'apart from me you can do nothing' (Jn 15:5). The spirit is willing, but the flesh is weak, O so weak!

> Give me the love that leads the way,
> The faith that nothing can dismay,

The hope no disappointments tire,
The passion that will burn like fire.
Let me not sink to be a clod:
Make me Thy fuel, Flame of God.

Amy Carmichael

9

It Happened to Me

In the last few years we have known of thousands of Christians receiving this promised power. They have known some power in their lives before. They have known about the Holy Spirit—but had little experience of him. They have drunk from the waters of life—but have never been deluged in the same waters. It has been thrilling to see person after person receive this promise by faith, and discover Christ is the same today as he was on the day of Pentecost, and gives the same gift with the same manifestation.

Permission has been granted to quote from some of the many letters we have received testifying to this transforming experience:

*   *   *

'I received the baptism of the Holy Spirit many years ago when I was a young curate. It is as fresh in my mind now as if it happened yesterday. Quite literally I walked with Christ. He was beside me. I could not turn my head to look at him, something seemed to prevent it. I wept tears of joy. This was years after the initial experience that converted me; that was something tremendous too. I knew nothing about tongues, but I had found myself able to make vocal sounds that meant nothing to me....'

'The whole of my communion with the Lord has suddenly acquired new dimensions. It was a little difficult at first...but the burden intensified until the Holy Spirit triumphed.... Often a matter is before me and the Spirit takes over in presenting it to God. Worship and adoration are wonderful and in the earlier phases especially confirmation was afforded that it was of the Lord.'

'There are now many of us among the young people of the district rejoicing in a new-found joy and peace in believing and evangelizing on the streets and in the coffee-bars of the district with a consuming fire in our bones that will not let us keep quiet...we are thrilled to be privileged to live in these exciting days of the latter rain. Truly there is no end to the riches available to us in our precious Lord! How wonderful Jesus is!'

'About eighteen months ago I had a rather shattering realization that I seemed to have no gospel to give to others, though I had a way for my own salvation. Then I heard Dennis Bennett on a tape. I came home and said to my wife, "This is it!" As time went on I became increasingly aware of gifts received from God—a new desire to read the Scriptures and a new realization of the meaning of faith and trust, a new relationship with others, a new freedom in the practice of disciplines,

almost with ease, which before had been laborious....
At last I can begin to say I have received the full
blessing. I have been filled with the Holy Spirit....'

'For the last three days now I have been able to "speak
in tongues"...with this gift of the Holy Spirit my life
has been affected as well. First, in a deep emotional
way. In my quiet time I have a sense of praying in
greater power in English after praying in another
tongue. There is a sense of peace and quiet joy, particularly after I have been practising the gift, and a
definite knowledge that it is Jesus giving the joy and I
am not just acknowledging it is from him because I am a
Christian.'

'Life is new and I rejoice—I can't remember when I was
last able to rejoice in such freedom. Nature dances and
people's eyes shine. Poetical? Yes, but metaphor and
the language of poetry is the inadequate best I can use
to describe the new creation which we now see.'

'How God came to bless me in this way is quite a long
story. In my quiet times he kept on bringing up
righteousness. He will lead, he will purge, he will
prune, and he will chasten. And in the meantime in
about four weeks I met five people who challenged me
on the baptism of the Holy Spirit. By the time the fifth
challenge came I knew God was speaking to me and I
received.... What has thrilled me more than anything
is now I begin to see Jesus. He is a reality.'

'I certainly never thought speaking in tongues was as
easy as that! Praise the Lord, I've found already that

the Lord is melting a heart of stone and putting love there instead. I just long to know the filling of the Spirit now, to receive all that God wants to give.... The Lord has been leading us all in a wonderful way as we have been praying for just this over the last three terms....'

'Since arriving in England I have met several old friends and new ones who have quite obviously received a special infilling from the Holy Spirit. Immediately they reminded me of some of the humble Christians among whom the Lord had sent me to work.... Here too was the same depth of faith and readiness to testify. As the Lord caused me to realize afresh my own impotence, I was filled with thanksgiving for the way he had kept me during five years, through earthquakes and floods, in perils and dangers, and had given me such joy in the work. He now showed me that there was more than this. On re-examining the New Testament record I was amazed at the change in the disciples from a handful of believers, yes, but unable to testify when the presence of the Lord has been removed... until his coming in a new and wonderful way in the person of his Holy Spirit. Had somebody asked me then, was I a Christian, I would have gladly said, "Yes, I have believed on the Lord Jesus." Had they then asked me if I had received the Holy Spirit, I would have changed the conversation, and continued questioning in my mind about these things. Since then the Lord has led me to wait on the Holy Spirit in a new way, and he has come into my life in a new way, with signs following as in the New Testament. Instead of being a burden, deputation work has been a time of sharing what the Lord has done... and is doing here.

The Lord is enabling me to testify by his Holy Spirit in a way which I could never have done before, and giving me a new joy and liberty in serving him....'

*   *   *

These are only a few testimonies, yet they cover a wide range of people—young and middle-aged, Evangelical and Anglo-Catholic, Anglican, Baptist and Brethren, ministers and lay people. God is re-equipping his church with the power of the Holy Spirit, so that it can go into action against a strong enemy. Sin and evil are so deeply entrenched in society today that nothing but our complete surrender to the full blessing of the Holy Spirit will enable us to make any impressive impact upon Satan's kingdom of darkness. We are only scratching the surface. Satan laughs at us.

We need all the weapons of God's armoury to be successful in this spiritual warfare. We may be different from the Ephesian disciples. We may have heard that there is a Holy Spirit. Our knowledge of him may be correct. But what of our experience of his power? The power is still available for the body of Christ and for each of its members. The Baptizer stands ready on the banks of the Holy Spirit to do again for the church what he did on the day of Pentecost.

Notes

1. *Fire upon the Earth* (Edinburgh House Press 1958), p. 79.
2. *The Household of God* (SCM Press 1953).
3. *The Path of Prayer* (Hodder & Stoughton 1968), p. 41.
4. Ibid., p. 41.
5. *The Path of Prayer* (Zondervan 1924), p. 134.
6. Ibid., p. 196.
7. *Autobiography of George Müller* (Pickering & Inglis 1929), pp. 33-34.
8. *St Matthew* (1940).
9. *A Castaway*, p. 86.
10. *The Holy Spirit, or Power from on High*, vol. 2 (Christian Alliance Publishing Company 1924), p. 21.
11. *The Person and Work of the Holy Spirit* (Fleming H. Revell 1910), pp. 174, 176.
12. *Lectures on the Ephesians* (Hodder & Stoughton 1895), p. 127.
13. *The Book of the Acts* (Marshall, Morgan & Scott 1962), p. 77.
14. Ibid., p. 181. Professor Bruce adds a touch of doubt by saying, "Whether the external signs which accompanied the gift of the Spirit on this occasion were identical with the Pentecostal signs or not, they were at any rate of so impressive a nature that Simon Magus craved the power to reproduce them at will" (p. 183).
15. *The Power of Prayer*, p. 169.
16. *Voice of Faith*, April 1964.
17. *The Gospel according to St John* (John Murray 1896), p. 123.

18. Hodder and Stoughton 1964.
19. *Revival, an Enquiry* (SCM Press).